THE LMS
IN
IRELAND

An Irish Railway Pictorial

Mark Kennedy

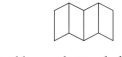

Midland Publishing

The LMS in Ireland
© Mark Lynd Kennedy 2000

ISBN 1 85780 097 4

Published by Midland Publishing
(an imprint of Ian Allan Publishing Ltd)
24 The Hollow, Earl Shilton
Leicester, LE9 7NA, England.
Tel: 01455 847 815 Fax: 01455 841 805
E-mail: midlandbooks@compuserve.com

Design concept and layout
© Midland Publishing and
Stephen Thompson Associates.

Printed in England by
Woolnough Bookbinding Limited
Irthlingborough, Northants, NN9 5SE.

Front cover: **Images that reflect aspects
of the company's varied activities in Ireland
surround the crest of the LMS.** Top left, then
clockwise: **A Railway Air Services DH.86 leaves
Belfast Harbour Airport (see page 91); W class
2-6-0 No 93, built in 1933 (see page 11);
Crewe-built tank No 6** *Holyhead* **of the DN&G
system (see page 62); An LMS turbine
steamer leaves for Scotland (see page 86).**

Title page: **There was more to the LMS in
Ireland than just the NCC lines of the former
Midland Railway in Ulster. The newly formed
company also inherited the Dundalk, Newry
& Greenore system, promoted, financed and
equipped by the London & North Western
Railway. Here, one of the line's Crewe-built
0-6-0 saddle tanks, No 1** *Macrory,* **is seen at
Greenore.** UFTM archive

CONTENTS

Chapter		Page
1	Broad Gauge Routes	6
2	The Narrow Gauge Lines	48
3	The LNWR Connection	60
4	At Peace and War	65
5	By Land, Sea and Air	80
6	The Post-War Era	92

INTRODUCTION

IN THE TRANSPORT ACT of 1919 the British government laid down that the best way forward for the country's railways was that they should be amalgamated into four large companies. When this occurred in 1923 the biggest of these, and one of the largest railway companies in the world at the time, was the London Midland & Scottish Railway. From its main termini in London at Euston and St Pancras, LMS tracks reached as far west as Swansea, south to Bournemouth, east to Lowestoft and to the far north of Scotland. The main constituents of the LMS were the London & North Western Railway and the Midland Railway and through these the LMS also inherited extensive railway interests in Ireland. Before looking at how those English companies came to be involved in Ireland it is essential to quickly examine the history of the railways of north-east Ulster in particular, in the second half of the nineteenth century.

The main railway serving the counties of Antrim and Londonderry was the Belfast & Northern Counties Railway. Its prosperity reflected that of north-east Ulster, much of which stemmed from the linen industry. A good deal of flax used to make linen was grown in County Londonderry and there were many mills in County Antrim to process it. The linen industry was helped by the American Civil War which caused a disruption in the supply of cotton, so increasing the demand for Irish linen. Luckily for the BNCR the area it served did not suffer the depopulation which was the fate of much of the rest of Ireland as a result of the Great Famine of the late 1840s.

The first railway to serve this area was the Belfast & Ballymena which opened on 11th April 1848 from Belfast to Ballymena, Randalstown and Carrickfergus. The line was built along the edge of Belfast Lough to Carrickfergus Junction, later renamed Greenisland, from where the Ballymena line ran north-west to Antrim. This meant that all main line trains had to reverse at Greenisland, a situation which pertained until the 1930s. The B&B was soon to be followed by the Ballymena, Ballymoney, Coleraine & Portrush Junction Railway whose first trains ran on 7th November 1855. This line made an end-on junction with the B&B at Ballymena and was taken over by that company on 1st January 1860. The next link connecting Belfast to the north-west was the Londonderry & Coleraine Railway which opened to passengers from Derry to Limavady in 1852 and to Coleraine in 1853. Through working between Derry and Belfast was not possible until 1860 when the bridge over the River Bann at Coleraine was completed.

The B&B changed its name in 1860 to the Belfast & Northern Counties Railway, reflecting the larger area which it was now serving. The BNCR took over the rolling stock of the L&CR in 1861 when it leased the line but it was another decade before the L&CR was acquired by the BNCR. At the other end of the system, an equally important line was added which was to generate much traffic over the years. The track from Carrickfergus was extended to Larne in 1862 by a separate company, the Carrickfergus & Larne Railway and shortly afterwards a steamer service began on the short sea crossing from Larne to Stranraer in south-west Scotland. The Carrickfergus & Larne Railway, which had been worked by the BNCR, was eventually acquired by its neighbour in 1890.

Away from what was to become the main line to Derry, the branch to Randalstown, which had opened at the same time as the Belfast to Ballymena line in April 1848, was extended to Cookstown in 1856. In 1880 the Derry Central Railway opened its 30 mile long line north from Magherafelt, on the Cookstown route, to Macfin Junction, about 5 miles south of Coleraine on the main line. The DCR followed this with a branch from Magherafelt to Draperstown in 1883. The BNCR, which had worked the Derry Central since it opened, acquired the line in 1901. A short branch off the former L&C line, to Limavady, which opened with that company's main line in 1853, was extended to Dungiven in 1883 by the Limavady & Dungiven Railway. All of these lines in time fell into the hands of the BNCR. A final broad gauge branch was added in 1884 by the BNCR itself, the four mile long line from Ballyclare Junction, on the Belfast to Derry line, to Ballyclare.

Up to the 1880s all the lines of the BNCR had been built to the Irish standard or broad gauge of 5ft 3in. However, Ireland's first narrow gauge lines had opened high in the glens of County Antrim in the 1870s. These had been promoted to tap reserves of iron ore. The distinction of being the first 3ft gauge line in the country went to the Glenariff Railway. This was purely a mineral line, built on private land and thus not needing an Act of Parliament. Opened in 1873, it closed in 1885. More relevant to our story was the Ballymena, Cushendall & Red Bay Railway. This narrow gauge line opened in 1875 and ran from Ballymena to an eventual terminus at Retreat, high in the glens overlooking Red Bay and Cushendall on the coast far below, though never actually reaching those places named in its title. A mineral line to start with, passenger services only commenced in 1886 following its takeover by the BNCR in 1884. The iron ore brought down from the hills had at first been transferred to broad gauge wagons for shipment to the coast.

On 1st August 1877, the first section of another 3ft gauge line was opened in County Antrim. This was the Ballymena & Larne Railway's line from Larne to Ballyclare. On 1st May 1884 a ¾ mile connection was opened, linking the BC&RB and B&L lines at Ballymena, which enabled mineral traffic to be taken through to the coast at Larne. The B&L line to Ballyclare was extended to Doagh in 1884 and the company was taken over by the BNCR in 1889.

Mineral traffic from the glens of Antrim had peaked by the time the BNCR took over the two narrow gauge lines radiating out from Ballymena. In an attempt to keep the erstwhile BC&RB in business a passenger service was started in 1888 to Parkmore, about 3 miles from the terminus at Retreat. Competition from road vehicles led to the closure of the line to passengers in 1930 though some goods traffic lingered on until 1940. On the B&L section, the branch to Doagh lost its passenger trains in 1930. Passenger services between Ballymena and Larne did not resume following a bitter strike in 1933 though goods trains continued to run from Larne to serve a paper mill at Ballyclare until 1950.

A further short narrow gauge line entered the BNCR fold in 1897. This was the Portstewart Tramway, which opened in 1882 to link Portstewart station, on the line between Coleraine and Portrush, with the town of Portstewart, some 1¾ miles away. By the 1920s the tramway was in poor order and it was closed in January 1926, the first 3ft gauge railway in Ireland to pass into history. A bus service replaced the steam trams. To complete this brief survey of the narrow gauge in north-east Ulster, mention must be made of the Ballycastle Railway. This 3ft gauge line was built by the independent BR in 1880 to link the seaside town of Ballycastle with the BNCR main line at Ballymoney, 16 miles away. The BR closed the line in March 1924 because of financial difficulties but it was rescued by the LMS and reopened in August of that year. Though almost the first of the Antrim narrow gauge lines to go, in the end it was the last one to close, services continuing until July 1950.

The English connection, which later led to these lines becoming part of the LMS, began in July 1903 when the Midland Railway (of England) purchased the BNCR. It inherited a mature and diverse business which consisted of 200 miles of broad gauge and 49 miles of narrow gauge track. The MR ran its Irish subsidiary through a committee based in Belfast known as the Northern Counties Committee. The day-to-day affairs of the railway and most executive decisions continued to be taken by the NCC in Belfast while the Midland collected the receipts and paid the bills. This arrangement was continued when the Midland Railway became part of the LMS in 1923.

The acquisitive Midland was keen to increase its Irish interests following the purchase of the BNCR. It turned its attention to the narrow gauge Donegal Railways which operated a network of lines connecting with the Great Northern Railway (Ireland) at Strabane in County Tyrone, on its alternative route to that operated by the NCC, from Belfast to Derry. The GNR, anxious to contain the MR's influence, agreed in 1906, to jointly purchase the DR with the Midland. A management group called the County Donegal Railways Joint Committee was set up to run these lines. The CDRJC pioneered the use of rail cars for its passenger services whilst maintaining a fleet of

steam locomotives for goods and excursion trains. The last CDR trains ran on New Year's Eve 1959, this part of the former LMS narrow gauge outlasting the lines in County Antrim.

In the 1930s, the financial strength of the LMS gave the NCC a cushion against the hard times that other railway companies in Ireland were having to endure. There was considerable investment in track, signalling, structures and in the locomotive fleet which, by the late 1940s, was the most modern of any railway in Ireland. Colour light signals were introduced

The NCC vigorously promoted tourism in Ulster with a series of attractive posters and brochures extolling the delights of the area it served. UFTM.

at Belfast and important junctions from the 1920s. The Greenisland loop line was opened in 1934 giving a direct run from Belfast to Antrim and beyond for the first time. The works involved a large concrete viaduct across Valentine's Glen near Whiteabbey, the down Larne line burrowing underneath it.

In 1933, a new design of express locomotive, the W class 2-6-0, was built at Derby to enable the NCC to run accelerated passenger and goods services over the new steeply graded Greenisland loop line. The engines were built using many standard LMS parts both for economy and ease of maintenance. Along with track improvements which allowed trains not scheduled to stop to run through passing loops on single line sections at speed, the new locomotives enabled the NCC to run some of the fastest schedules ever afforded by steam traction in Ireland. The punctuality of NCC trains during the 1930s was exemplary.

When the Belfast & Ballymena Railway opened in 1848 it had 11 engines. By 1861 the BNCR owned 34 locomotives. All locomotives built between 1890 and 1908 were compounds, but most were later rebuilt to simple engines. Compounds continued to be built for the narrow gauge until 1920. Most NCC locos of the period were either 2-4-0 or 4-4-0 tender engines. Standardisation of engines began in the early 1920s with the use of MR type boilers. The LMS continued this policy. Carriages produced for the NCC also depended heavily on the designs of the MR works at Derby, most having similar characteristics to the MR or LMS vehicles of the time. Passenger carriage stock consisted of around 180 broad gauge vehicles.

Having taken the story of the NCC up to the 1930s, it is now time to reflect on the other element of LMS involvement in the Irish railway scene, which came with the lines owned before grouping by the LNWR. From the 1840s onwards the LNWR was heavily involved with the conveyance of goods and passengers to Ireland with its acquisition of the Chester & Holyhead Railway. The oldest named train in the world was the LNWR's 'Irish Mail' which ran between Euston and Holyhead. Anxious to increase its share of the lucrative Irish traffic, in the 1870s the company became heavily involved financially with a nominally independent Irish company, the Dundalk, Newry & Greenore Railway. Its aim was to develop a port for cross channel traffic at Greenore in County Louth and build two railway lines to connect it to Newry and Dundalk.

The line from Greenore to Dundalk was the first to open in 1873 and this was followed by the line to Newry in 1876. The port and the railways were never very successful and passenger steamers ceased to run in 1926. What was remarkable about the DN&G was that even down to such details as signals and the colour of its tickets, it was like a part of the LNWR which had somehow been moved across the Irish Sea. Rolling stock consisted of Crewe-built 0-6-0 saddle tank locomotives dating from the 1870s and the six-wheel carriages continued to carry authentic LNWR livery right up to the lines' closure in 1951.

When Ireland was partitioned in 1922, the port of Greenore and most of its connecting railways were in the newly created Irish Free State. The imposition of the border cutting across established trading patterns, which the railways had been built to reflect and support, did little to help the prosperity of these and many other cross border lines. Although freight and cattle traffic on the steamers working out of Greenore remained fairly healthy, the railways were no longer profitable. In order to achieve economies, in 1933 the LMS passed over the working of the DNGR lines to the Great Northern Railway, in the heart of whose territory the system was located. Though some GNR locos appeared on services, the LNWR saddle tanks and their matching six-wheelers remained active until the lines closed, an LNWR time warp on the wrong side of the Irish Sea.

Above: **The NCC, like other Irish railways experimented with railbuses. No 42, pauses between duties at Waterside station in Londonderry (see also page 65).**
Midland Publishing collection

At the same time as they were involved with the lines centred on Greenore and again in pursuit of an increased share of traffic across the Irish Sea, the LNWR built its own station at its steamer berth on the North Wall in Dublin. A passenger station, hotel and a goods and cattle yard were built. In 1877 a short branch was opened to link the LNWR's facilities to Church Road Junction from where connections were made to the GNR, Great Southern & Western and Midland Great Western systems. Passenger trains, providing connections off LNWR steamers to Dublin's other stations, ran until 1922.

In the late 19th century the LNWR also invested in various projects promoted by the Dublin, Wicklow & Wexford Railway, which changed its name in 1907, to the Dublin & South Eastern. These investments were designed in the main to keep the Great Western Railway excluded from a share in the Irish Sea traffic. With the development of the ports of Fishguard and Rosslare in the early years of the twentieth century, these financial involvements ultimately failed to achieve that objective.

One legacy from these investments did affect the LMS on its formation. Under a clause in an Act of Parliament obtained by the DW&W in 1870, the LNWR was allowed to appoint a director to the board of that company. The LNWR's representative in 1921 on the DSER board was the Rt Hon Henry Givens Burgess, who was ultimately to become the General Manager of the LMS. In 1923 the government of the Irish Free State, like the British government across the Irish Sea, was pressing for the amalgamation of the railway companies within its jurisdiction. One sticking point in the negotiations leading to the Irish grouping was the seat which the newly formed LMS had inherited from the LNWR, on the board of the DSER. The LMS not unreasonably argued that they should either have a repayment of the £100,000

which the LNWR had invested in the DW&W or a seat on the board of the new merged Irish railway company. The matter was finally resolved and when the Great Southern Railways, as the new company was called, came into existence on 1st January 1925, Burgess had a seat on its board representing the interests of the LMS.

The 1930s represented the heyday of NCC main line passenger services. This was epitomised by the named expresses such as 'The Portrush Flyer' and 'The North Atlantic Express'. Formed of modern LMS coaches hauled by the new Derby-built 2-6-0s, some of these trains had schedules of a mile per minute for part of their journeys.

By this time however, road haulage was beginning to adversely impact the railway companies. The NCC responded, not just with fast express timings, but by introducing competitively priced door-to-door deliveries for goods. Under the dynamic leadership of Malcolm Speir, its Scottish Manager and Secretary who came to Ulster in 1931, the NCC made great efforts to become a more broadly based transport company and not just a railway operator.

From the beginnings of the railway, horse drawn omnibuses provided feeder services to many stations. On 1st April 1902 the BNCR became the first railway in Ireland to use mechanically propelled vehicles for passenger road services and in 1905 it acquired two Thornycroft charabancs for use on tours. However, the NCC did not become a large-scale bus operator until after the passing of the Railway (Road Vehicles) NI Act in 1927, when, with the financial resources of the LMS behind it, the NCC began to build up a transport monopoly throughout its territory. In 1930, the NCC opened a central bus depot at Smithfield in Belfast housing 40 buses. The following year, the company introduced formal bus stops whereas previously vehicles would have stopped anywhere. Another innovation was tickets interchangeable between the company's road and rail services. The NCC operated bus services covering a route mileage of about 565 miles, practically double that of its railways. The company standardised its fleet by purchasing mainly Leyland and Albion buses.

By 1935, the NCC was the second largest passenger road operator in the province and owned 131 buses.

Unrestricted competition between rail and road led the government to pass the Northern Ireland Road and Rail Act of 1935 in which the operation of all public road services in the province was entrusted to the newly created Northern Ireland Road Transport Board. The NCC road fleet was compulsorily acquired by the NIRTB in exchange for shares in the new company. Unfortunately the NIRTB failed to co-operate with the railways as it was supposed to, and in many cases, NIRTB buses began to compete directly with railway passenger services. With the NCC and the other railway companies barred from operating road vehicles under the 1935 Act, there was no way they could counter this threat.

The NCC was innovative in exploring new ways to operate its railways. It experimented with railcars throughout the first half of the twentieth century. The earliest steam railcars entered service in 1905. A petrol omnibus was converted to run on rails in 1924 and the company's first modern railcar was introduced in 1933 with three more appearing before the Second World War. In addition, several diesel shunting locomotives made by the Belfast ship builders, Harland & Wolff, were acquired by the NCC.

The NCC played an important role during the Second World War as it was strategically placed to serve ports and factories which were crucial to the war effort. Even before the hostilities had begun, the NCC prepared an emergency skeleton timetable and built air-raid shelters. Engines and carriages were fitted with blackout blinds, at stations all glass roofs were painted black and name boards were removed. The NCC reduced its speeds from the outbreak of war and withdrew many local services.

It was thought that Belfast was out of the range of German bombers but the Luftwaffe had other plans. They bombed the poorly defended city on the night of 7-8th April 1941, causing damage to the docks and destroying an aircraft fuselage factory at Harland & Wolff. A week later, on the night of Easter Tuesday 15th April, 180 Heinkel and Junkers bombers returned. Officially there were 745 people killed and 430 seriously injured, although it is thought that at least 900 people died that night. No other UK city outside London lost so many people in a single raid. The NCC was badly hit, its offices and stores were destroyed and York Road station was badly damaged. On the evening of Sunday 4th May the bombers returned again and managed to destroy the rest of the office accommodation, goods sheds and repair shops. York Road station's roof caught fire and collapsed on twenty carriages parked underneath, gutting them.

In 1946 the LMS made its final lasting contribution to its railways in Ulster when the first four of a batch of eighteen 2-6-4 tank locomotives were delivered from Derby. Based on the W class 2-6-0 tender engines of the 1930s, the new tanks quickly acquired the nickname of 'Jeeps', a reflection of their ruggedness and reliability. The Jeeps lasted until the end of steam in Ireland. A number were retained into the early 1970s to haul trains of spoil from a quarry at Magheramorne to Belfast to build the M2 motorway. The handful of Jeeps which survived for these workings were among the last steam locomotives to run in railway company service in these islands.

On 1st January 1948, the LMS was taken over by the British Transport Commission Railway Executive to become part of the nationalised British Railways. The Northern Ireland government also determined to nationalise public transport at this time and set up the Ulster Transport Authority, giving it responsibility for the co-ordination of public transport in Northern Ireland. The British Transport Commission sold the NCC to the UTA for £2,668,000 in December 1948, the transfer of ownership, taking place on 1st April 1949.

The UTA, reviled to this day by those who care about railways, was run by people with a bias towards road transport and almost at once embarked on an orgy of closures. By the end of the 1950s, of the former LMS-NCC network, only the lines serving Larne, Portrush and Londonderry, were still open.

In the pages which follow we will explore many aspects of LMS involvement in Ireland. In addition to the trains, we will examine the company's shipping routes on the Irish Sea, bus services, hotels and the development of tourism and even the railway air services which operated between the wars. Much may have been lost over the years but the impressive contribution which the LMS made to Ireland in the years during which the company was in existence, deserves to be put on record.

ACKNOWLEDGEMENTS

Anyone researching the NCC must pay tribute to the work of Mac Arnold, Harold Houston and Russell Currie, without whose efforts our knowledge of the system would be much the poorer. In the case of this book, I am particularly indebted to Charles Friel for his help.

In addition thanks are due to the following individuals and organisations who have helped me in the course of my researches: Andrew Anderson, Chris Aspinwall, Ed Bartholmew, William Coates, Michael Collins, Dr Bill Crawford, the Downpatrick Steam Railway, Frank Dunlop, Alan Edgar, Tom Ferris, Clifton Flewitt, Johnny and Will Glendinning, Stephen Goodhand of Hull Transport Museum, David Henderson, Colin Holliday, the Imperial War Museum, the Irish Railway Record Society, Major Eric Kirby, John Lockett, the Locomotive Club of Great Britain, John Mc Guigan, Michael Mc Mahon, D B McNeill, Alfred Montgomery, William Montgomery, Lawrence Morrison, David Mosley of the National Railway Museum, the Museums and Galleries of Northern Ireland, the Railway Preservation Society of Ireland, Herbert Richards, Mike Rutherford, Chris Salter, Peter Scott, Sally Skilling, John Stroud for his help with the section dealing with the Railway Air Services, Steve Thompson, the Ulster Folk & Transport Museum and the Friends of Cultra, the Ulster Museum, Debra Wenlock and Jack Woods.

Finally I would like to extend my special thanks to Maureen Paige and the photographic department of the Ulster Folk & Transport Museum. Many of the images used in the book have come from the UFTM's archives. The reference numbers for these pictures are prefixed by the letters UFTM throughout the book .

Mark Kennedy, Bangor   August 2000

Below: **Some of the men of the NCC, who worked in the fitting shop at York Road, pose for their works photo in 1933, in front of their latest locomotive, one of the first of the W class 2-6-0s.** UFTM L3313/8

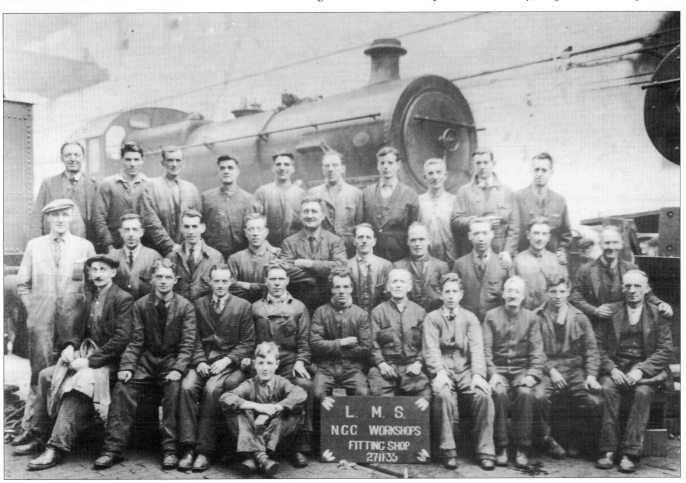

BROAD GAUGE ROUTES

Above: **An Austin taxi is seen waiting at the bus stop outside York Road station in the mid-1930s. Bus stops were an innovation introduced in Belfast by NCC road services** in 1931. Before this, buses had stopped anywhere on request to pick up or set down passengers. UFTM L4192/7

YORK ROAD STATION

We begin our travels along the broad gauge routes of the NCC at the place where many such journeys began, York Road station in Belfast. The company's main terminus was located on the corner of York Road and Whitla Street, not too far from the city centre. The station was close to the shores of Belfast Lough and was built partly on reclaimed land. The premises also included the Midland Hotel which was popular both with businessmen and tourists. From York Road the line ran parallel with the Lough to near Whiteabbey. Level at first, it then began to climb away from the shore to cross the viaducts over Valentine's Glen at Bleach Green, where the Larne line branched off from the main line to Portrush and Londonderry. There is a continuous uphill gradient of 1 in 75 for the three miles from Whiteabbey to Monkstown. From there the line continued north-west past Kingsbog Junction, the highest point on the NCC's broad gauge system, where the branch to Ballyclare diverged. The next important station was Antrim, where the GNR line from Knockmore Junction near Lisburn, trailed in from the south. At Cookstown Junction, just over three miles beyond Antrim, the line to Magherafelt and Cookstown left the main line. The Derry Central struck off from this line at Magherafelt to rejoin the main line at Macfin, not far from Coleraine. The NCC main line continued through Ballymena and Ballymoney to Coleraine where it divided with a branch going off to Portrush. Between Coleraine and Londonderry, at Limavady Junction, the final broad gauge branch, that from Dungiven and Limavady joined the main line which terminated at Waterside station in Derry, some 95 miles from York Road.

Left: **York Road and Queen's Quay stations, the latter the city terminus of the Belfast & County Down Railway, were unusual in that they had tram tracks running right on to their concourses, an arrangement which was very convenient for passengers. Two Belfast Corporation electric tram cars are seen inside York Road about 1930.**
UFTM L1403/1/34a

Above: **The passenger concourse of the NCC's Belfast headquarters is seen in this view dating from May 1899. The station had been greatly extended in the 1890s under the direction of Berkeley Deane Wise. York Road station suffered considerable damage from air raids during the Second World War. It was to suffer more bomb damage in 1970, during Northern Ireland's more recent troubles. The chalet-style book and tobacco stall has survived and can be seen, minus its clock tower, in the Transport Gallery at the Ulster Folk and Transport Museum at Cultra. The other clocks, to the left of the picture, had no working mechanism. Their hands were set by staff to show the departure time of the next train whose destination was indicated by a board beside the clock face.**
UFTM L436/1

Right: **U2 class 4-4-0 No 83 *Carra Castle*, is blowing off steam, prior to departure at Belfast York Road station, in the Autumn of 1932. It was built by the North British Locomotive Company of Glasgow, entering service in May 1925, but was not given its name until 1932. The headlamp code indicates to signalmen that this train is bound for the Larne branch. 'Castle' class engines usually hauled the Boat trains on the Larne line at this time and had to cover the 24¼ miles between Belfast and Larne Harbour in 30 minutes, a timing which called for some very smart running. No 83 was withdrawn by the UTA in 1956.**
Northern Whig and *Belfast Post*: UFTM L3535/23

Left: **Motorway building since the 1970s has radically altered this part of Belfast. York Road station had five platforms, all of which could be used for either the arrival or departure of trains. Platform four was the longest at 609ft. Contrary to usual practice, the middle roads had no cross-overs at the buffer stop ends to allow the release of engines from arriving trains. The middle lines were used to house empty stock. Today the M2 motorway runs parallel with the main line which now continues past the site of the terminal station to the new Yorkgate station, before continuing across the River Lagan to reach Belfast Central station. This view dates from the late 1940s.** Reg Ludgate collection: UFTM LUD 2505

Below: **Looking in the other direction, the engine shed and its large LMS era coaling plant can be seen in this early 1950s picture.** Reg Ludgate collection: UFTM LUD 2504

YORK ROAD WORKS

Top: The NCC's workshops were located at York Road. Locomotive No 21 is seen in the erecting shop at the works in 1930. This engine was built in 1890 by Beyer Peacock as a 2-4-0, one of the seven C class locos supplied between 1890 and 1895. Its original number was 51. It was rebuilt in 1926 as a B1 class 4-4-0 and renumbered 21 in 1928 during a second rebuild which equipped it with an LMS G6 type superheated boiler. It was named *County Down* in July 1932 and finally withdrawn in June 1947. J H Houston: UFTM L3739/11

Lower left: The **wheel lathe at the works, capable of machining the largest driving wheels, towers over a member of staff.** J H Houston: UFTML4197/12

Lower right: **A general view of the erecting shop at York Road works in 1936 showing the line shaft driven press, rolling machine and forge. To the rear of the building is an ADC bus chassis, registration number XI 9633, in the process of being converted into a lorry for use on the NCC's door-to-door haulage service.** J H Houston collection: UFTM L3739/10

Top: **Some locomotives were built as well as repaired at York Road works. Class U2 4-4-0 tender loco No 81 *Carrickfergus Castle* was built there in 1925. Seen here at Belfast in the late 1930s, it received its name in December 1930 and remained in service until 1957.** J H Houston: UFTM MS553

Lower left: **This view dating from 1934 shows two of the new W class 2-6-0s being assembled and railcar No 2 under construction. The two Moguls which entered service in that year were Nos 94 and 95. This shop is still used today by Northern Ireland Railways. The two 40-ton overhead cranes were supplied by Herbert Morris Limited of Loughborough.**
Belfast Telegraph collection: UFTM L3354/11

Lower right: **Class D two cylinder Worsdell von Borries compound locomotive No 55 *Parkmount* undergoing repairs at York Road works in August 1930. This engine was built for the BNCR in 1895 by Beyer Peacock during the long period when compound locomotives were very much in favour on the system. Though built as a 2-4-0, No 55 was rebuilt as a 4-4-0 as early as 1897, in which form it lasted until the early 1940s.** H C Casserley: UFTM L4192/9

YORK ROAD DEPARTURES

Right: **The Londonderry Mail train leaving Belfast on 16th September 1909.**
The small tank engine hauled the train to Greenisland, 6 miles from Belfast, where it was replaced by a main line locomotive which backed on at the other end of the train for the run to Derry. K A C R Nunn, Locomotive Club of Great Britain: UFTM L4191/1

Centre: **B class 4-4-0 No 24, seen leaving Belfast York Road with a Greenisland train in September 1934, was built as a compound by Beyer Peacock for the BNCR in 1898. It was rebuilt in 1925 as a simple and given the name *County Londonderry* in 1932. It was withdrawn in 1947.**
Rail Archive Stephenson: QP1572

Below: **NCC W class 2-6-0 No 93 at Belfast York Road with an express for Londonderry in September 1934. This was one of the first batch of four Moguls which were supplied the previous year. It did not receive its name, *The Foyle*, until 1936.**
Rail Archive Stephenson: QP1586

Left: **U1 class 4-4-0 No 1 at Belfast York Road in the 1920s before the semaphore signals at the station were replaced by colour lights. No 1 was built in 1924 at York Road, named *Glenshesk* in June 1932 and withdrawn in April 1947. A number of the older tender engines were taken out of service at this time to make way for the new WT class 2-6-4 tanks. Prior to 1924 the NCC engines were painted in a livery known as 'invisible green', which looked like black to most observers. They were lined out in yellow, blue and vermillion. This colour scheme was replaced by the crimson lake livery used by the LMS across the water.** J H Houston: UFTM MS541

Above: **No 50 *Jubilee*, seen at York Road in 1937, was a sister locomotive of No 55 (see page 10) and had the same varied career. Built by Beyer Peacock in 1895 as a 2-4-0 compound, it was rebuilt as a 4-4-0 in 1897. This locomotive lasted until 1946. Their 7ft driving wheels were the largest used by the BNCR.** Midland Publishing collection

Left: **By the 1950s most of the old loco-motives had been withdrawn and services were largely in the hands of the W and WT classes. On 14th April 1955 Mogul No 101, *Lord Masserene*, leaves York Road with a main line working.** H C Casserley

BLEACH GREEN

Above: **The viaducts at Bleach Green, built in the early 1930s, are the most striking feature of the climb out from York Road. They transformed services on the NCC and ushered in the fast timings of the pre war years. In this 1948 view, a down Larne train has just passed under the main line viaduct in the background. The loco is by No 28, a diesel electric, built by Harland & Wolff in 1937 for the BCDR.**
Harland & Wolff collection: UFTM 11863

THE BALLYCLARE BRANCH

Above right: **A 4-4-0 locomotive and a train consisting of a solitary brake carriage are seen at Ballyclare Junction in 1936 on a Ballyclare to Belfast working. This station was about a mile from the actual divergence of the four mile long branch, which closed completely in July 1950.**
Charles Friel collection: UFTM L4191/2

Right: **Railcar No 1, built in 1933 and powered by two Leyland petrol engines, seen here at Ballyclare, probably offered ample accommodation for the passenger traffic on the branch.**
Reg Ludgate collection: UFTM LUD 2543

ANTRIM

Left: **The main station building at Antrim was designed by Wise and built in 1901/2. Its overall appearance is similar to a large double bay house in the mock Tudor style. The arched entrance on the down platform leads through to a red brick block on the platform side. Ornamental cast iron columns support the glazed roof of the platform canopy. There was also an impressive pedestrian footbridge supplied by the Saracen Foundry of Glasgow. The station building jointly served the NCC and the Great Northern Railway.**
R Welch: UFTM L4107/5

Above: **The 9.45am Belfast to Londonderry train, headed by W class 2-6-0 No 92, pauses at Antrim station on Friday 29th June 1934. This was one of the first of the new Moguls which entered service the previous year. It was named, *The Bann*, in 1936.** William Robb: UFTM L4191/3

Left: **In UTA days, U2 class 4-4-0 No 80, is seen leaving Antrim for Ballymena. Built by the NCC in 1925 and named *Dunseverick Castle* in 1933, these engines were capable of achieving speeds of over 70mph on fast trains to Portrush.** UFTM L3539/2

THE DERRY CENTRAL LINES

Top: **Loco No 75 at Cookstown Junction shed on 10th August 1937.** Two engines had been based here until the strike of 1933 when the shed was closed as an economy measure. The windmill pumped water for the engines into the water tower. When originally opened in 1848, it was known as Drumsough but was renamed Cookstown Junction in November 1856. It reverted to Drumsough again in 1976. The photographer is looking towards Derry, the Cookstown branch is on the left hand side of the engine shed. There were eleven NCC sheds. Their allocations on 1st January 1932 were as follows, the number of locos at each shed is shown in brackets; Belfast (28), Whitehead (1), Larne (5 broad gauge, 6 narrow gauge), Cookstown Junction (2), Ballymena (6 broad gauge, 2 narrow gauge), Coleraine (6), Londonderry (4), Magherafelt (2), Cookstown (1), Limavady (1), Ballycastle (2 narrow gauge). In addition eleven engines were under or awaiting repair. This gives a grand total of 77 engines on the company's books at this time. W A Camwell: UFTM L4191/4

Centre: **U2 class locomotive No 81** is crossing Randalstown viaduct, heading for Belfast, on 12th August 1938. This eight-span masonry viaduct over the River *Maine* opened in 1856 and still dominates the town long after the closure of the railway. It is now used as a public footpath and is illuminated at night.
William Robb: UFTM L4191/13

Bottom: **Locomotive No 78 *Chichester Castle*** on the 6.39pm service from Cookstown Junction to Cookstown is seen at Magherafelt on 27th June 1950. The 5.30pm Portrush to Antrim service via the Derry Central line is at the other platform. Passenger services on the Derry Central line finished on 28th August 1950.
J Edgington: UFTM LUD 2503

Top left: **At Magherafelt, where the Cookstown line branched off from the Derry Central route, class A compound No 65, built in 1905 by the Midland Railway, is shunting a brake van at the station. This locomotive was rebuilt in 1929 as a class A1 simple engine and named** *Knockagh* **in 1931. It was withdrawn in 1950 by the UTA. The station notice boards display posters encouraging the public to properly label their luggage.** Charles Friel collection: UFTM L4191/12

Below left: **A mile from Magherafelt station, just beyond bridge No 305, was Draperstown Junction. Seen through the bridge, the Draperstown line diverges to the right off the Cookstown line.** Charles Friel collection: UFTM L4192/1

Above right: **Locomotive No 65 and a brake van arrive at Desertmartin, the only intermediate station on the Draperstown branch. This line opened in 1883, lost its passenger services in 1930 and closed completely in 1950.** Charles Friel collection: UFTM L4192/2

Left: **U2 class 4-4-0 No 79** *Kenbaan Castle* **calls at Aghadowey, some 25 miles from Magherafelt, with the morning Magherafelt to Coleraine passenger train along the Derry Central line, on 30th March 1950. Two months later this engine was sent to the former BCDR Queen's Quay works for overhaul. The rebuild had to be completed at York Road when the County Down workshops were closed by the UTA later the same year.** UFTM L1525/1

COOKSTOWN

Right: **Cookstown was 27 miles from Cookstown Junction. The GNR station is on the left and the NCC one is to the right in this 1936 view.** Charles Friel collection: UFTM L4191/16

Centre right: **Class C 2-4-0 No 51 waits at the platform at Cookstown. This engine was built by Beyer Peacock in 1890 and was experimentally converted to burn oil in November 1896 using Holden's Patent Oil Burning Apparatus. It was converted back to coal firing after five years as an oil burner.** Charles Friel collection: UFTM L4191/15

Bottom: **Class C1 locomotive No 57, *Galgorm Castle*, at Cookstown with the 12.40pm to Belfast on a snowy day in December 1935, three years before it was withdrawn. In 1908, No 57 became the first locomotive in the world to be fitted with a Ross 'Pop' safety valve. This was made at Coleraine shed by R L Ross who worked as a fitter there. The type became widely used elsewhere by the 1920s. The advantage of the Ross valve was the small pressure difference, only 1-2lb per sq in, between opening and closing, compared with other designs such as the Ramsbottom valve, where the difference was over 5lb per sq in. This of course meant that less steam was wasted when a locomotive fitted with a Ross valve blew off.** O S Nock, Charles Friel collection: UFTM L4191/14

BALLYMENA

Top: **After our excursion to Cookstown and along the Derry Central line, we pick up the NCC main line again at Ballymena, where a pair of NCC 4-4-0s, class U2 No 82 *Dunananie Castle* and class U1 No 1 *Glenshesk,* are seen at the station. The goods yard and the narrow gauge line to Retreat are behind the signal cabin.**
C H Hewison: UFTM L4191/5

Lower left: **Mogul No 93 *The Foyle,* leaves Ballymena with the 2.25pm Belfast to Derry train on 10th August 1938.**
William Robb: UFTM L4191/7

Lower right: **The pioneering NCC railcar No 1 was recorded hauling a carriage at Ballymena in 1933. No 1 was later limited to drawing vehicles weighing a maximum of 15 to 20 tons depending on the route. The man leaning out the cab window is the NCC's Locomotive and Civil Engineer, Hugh P Stewart, who retired that year.**
Charles Friel collection: UFTM L4191/6

Opposite page

Top: **A fine portrait of W class 2-6-0 No 95 *The Braid* at Ballymena on an up goods train, taken in early 1936. The locomotive is in LMS crimson lake livery and is paired with a small tender which does not suit the proportions of the locomotive. Tablet catching equipment, a distinctive NCC cast number plate and an LMS crest adorn the cabside of the locomotive.**
O S Nock, Charles Friel collection

BALLYMONEY

Below: **The next major town served by the NCC main line was Ballymoney, some 20** miles on from Ballymena. **This was the junction for the narrow gauge line to Ballycastle which terminated on the other side of the up main line platform. The sight of trains on Ireland's two main gauges alongside each other at Ballymoney was not going to last much longer when this** view was taken on 20th May 1950. No 100 *Queen Elizabeth* **arrives with a train from Belfast as S1 class 2-4-2 tank No 41 waits on the other side of the platform with the connecting service to Ballycastle. The line closed on 3rd July 1950.**
W H G Boot: UFTM L4191/8

COLERAINE

Top: **U2 class 4-4-0 No 77, built in 1924 by the North British Locomotive Company in Glasgow, is seen shunting cattle wagons at Coleraine on 27th June 1950.**
J Edgington: UFTM LUD 2500

Centre: **The first railway to reach Coleraine was the Londonderry & Coleraine which began services to a station on the west bank of the River Bann in July 1853. The line from Belfast opened in December 1855 and continued through to Portrush, but it was not until November 1860 that a bridge over the river was opened linking the two lines and allowing through running from Belfast to Derry. The first bridge was replaced by a new structure which opened in 1924 This photograph was taken at the opening ceremony on 24th March of that year, with assorted dignitaries posing for the camera in front of the opening section of the bridge which is raised behind them as a backdrop for the photograph. This was the first Strauss under-hung counterweight bascule lifting bridge to be erected in these islands.** Welch Studios: UFTM L3535/24

Bottom: **A short branch down to Coleraine Harbour was opened in 1892. Constructed by Coleraine Harbour Commissioners, it joined the main line just outside the station where the Portrush branch also diverged. In this view dating from the 1920s, NCC goods wagons are at the quay side and Coleraine's old and new railway bridges can be seen in the background. The ship in the foreground is *Briarthorn*, built in 1910 by A Hall of Aberdeen. It was owned by W J Ireland and registered in Liverpool.** W A Green: UFTM WAG 2190

PORTRUSH

Above: **The line to the holiday resort of Portrush was an important source of traffic for the NCC. With its own named expresses in the 1930s, it shared equal billing with the main line to Derry. The mock Tudor station building at Portrush was built by** McLaughlin & Harvey, to the design of Berkeley Deane Wise, and opened in the Spring of 1893. It replaced the original 1855 structure, which had become inadequate to deal with the summer excursion traffic. The wing on the right of the building housed a café and restaurant. Underneath the restaurant were large cellars used to store liquor for the railway's hotels, dining cars and refreshment rooms. Electric trams from the Giant's Causeway terminated to the left of the station.
W A Green: UFTM WAG 364

Below: **A siding opened in 1866 from Portrush station to the harbour. From 1883 to 1895 this had mixed gauge tracks to accomodate the 3ft gauge Giant's Causeway Tramway's goods traffic to the harbour.**
W A Green: UFTM WAG 360

Left: **U2 class No 75 built in 1924 by the North British Locomotive Co, was named** *Antrim Castle* **in 1931, and is pictured at Portrush in the 1930s.** UFTM L3538/12

Centre: **Mogul No 97** *Earl of Ulster,* **with the 2.50pm train to Belfast, is about to depart from Portrush on 10th August 1938.** William Robb: UFTM L4192/6

Bottom: **No 63, an A class two cylinder compound built at Derby in 1905, is seen here leaving Portrush in the mid 1920s. It was named** *Queen Alexandra* **in 1932 and withdrawn in 1936.** National Railway Museum York: 84/3007

Above: **The most scenic stretch of the NCC main line was that between Castlerock and Downhill where the track ran close to the coast. U2 class 4-4-0 No 77 is seen emerging from one of the tunnels on this section in the early UTA era. The wagon with sliding doors next to the engine was known as a 'brown van', so called because of its livery. These high capacity, vacuum braked vans, some of which were built by Harland & Wolff, were extensively used on NCC passenger trains.**
Reg Ludgate collection: UFTM LUD 2507

Right: **Above Downhill tunnel stood the Mussenden Temple. This was built in the eighteenth century by Frederick Hervey, the flamboyant Earl Bishop of Derry, as a memorial to his young cousin Frideswade Mussenden. Modelled on the Temple of Vesta in Italy and used as a library, it is now a National Trust property.**
W A Green: UFTM WAG 184

Top left: **Continuing our journey along the NCC main line, we see WT class 2-6-4 tank No 3, with the 2.40pm express from Belfast to Derry, passing Umbra between Downhill and Magilligan.** Drew Donaldson: UFTM L4191/9

Centre left: **Magilligan station, in this view looking towards Derry, was opened by the L&C in 1853. A tramway from here to Magilligan Point was opened in 1855 but only lasted a few months. The station building has recently been renovated and converted into apartments.** Reg Ludgate collection: UFTM LUD 2501

Bottom: **WT tank No 52 heads the 1.15pm Belfast to Derry service at Limavady Junction on 27th June 1950. At the other platform is A1 class 4-4-0 No 58 on the connection to Limavady. The passenger service to Limavady ended a week later on 3rd July. The somersault signal to the right of the locomotive is a repeater which replicated the aspect of the main signal at the top of the signal post for the benefit of drivers whose view of the signal might have been obscured by the station fotbridge. The L&C line reached Limavady in 1852. When construction resumed towards Coleraine it was from what became Limavady Junction, leaving the town of Limavady on a branch over three miles from the main line. In 1883 the branch was extended ten miles to serve Dungiven, by a nominally separate company, the Limavady & Dungiven Railway.** J Edgington: UFTM LUD 2502

THE DUNGIVEN BRANCH

Right: **The first station on the branch to Limavady and Dungiven was Broighter, which was less than a mile from the junction. Passenger services between Limavady and Dungiven were withdrawn in 1933 though the line remained open for goods until 1950. After withdrawal of passenger services between Limavady and the main line in 1950, that part of the branch remained open for goods traffic until May 1955.** Charles Friel collection: UFTM L4192/3

Above: **U1 class 4-4-0 No 4A *Glenariff* at Limavady on 22nd April 1948. It was given the suffix 'A' to avoid confusion with a new WT tank locomotive with the same number which had been delivered from Derby the previous year. Any confusion which this could have caused would have been short lived as No 4A was withdrawn in 1949.** H C Casserley: UFTM L4192/4

Right: **Recorded after the withdrawal of passenger services to Dungiven, B3 class No 21 *County Down*, rests at the buffer stops at the terminus whilst working the branch goods.** Charles Friel collection: UFTM L4192/5

LONDONDERRY WATERSIDE

Right: **Londonderry Waterside station was built in 1873/75 when it replaced an earlier structure which had been built for the opening of the line in 1852. This handsome building in dressed stone with an Italianate tower provided good passenger accommodation with the two platforms** sheltered by an overall roof. It was quite different in style from the other stations on the Derry to Coleraine line, most of which were finished in red brick. Though still in existence, it was replaced by an austere modern station, some 200 yards to the west, in 1980. UFTM L3475/6

Below: **U2 class 4-4-0 No 73 is seen inside the train shed at Londonderry Waterside in 1936.** O 3 Nock, Charles Friel collection; UFTM L4191/10

Left: **A view from the end of the platforms on a foggy day in the 1930s. The engine shed is to the left of the locomotive and part of the goods yard can be seen to the right of the distinctive BNCR somersault signals. There was a mixed gauge siding from the goods yard that ran through to the CDR's Victoria Road station, which was on the same side of the River Foyle beyond the city's Craigavon bridge. Further mixed gauge tracks ran along the bottom deck of the bridge. By means of turntables, wagons could be winched and manhandled across the river providing a tenuous connection with Derry's other two stations on the west bank of the Foyle. U2 class No 77, the locomotive in the picture, was designed by Henry Fowler of the LMS and W K Wallace of the NCC. It had an LMS G7 type boiler.**
Charles Friel collection: UFTM L4101/7

THE LARNE LINE

Above: **Having followed the course of the NCC main line to Londonderry, we retrace our steps to explore the line to Larne. This was always more than just another branch. The line had double track as far as Whitehead and its terminus at Larne Harbour was one of the major ports of the north of Ireland. Since the line opened in the 1860s steamer services on the short sea** route to Stranraer in the south-west of Scotland brought a steady stream of goods and passenger traffic to the line. The first part of the route, from Belfast to Carrickfergus, was opened by the B&B in April 1848, the rest of the line to Larne Harbour was built by the Carrickfergus & Larne Railway by October 1862. The point of divergence for the Larne line since 1934 has been Bleach Green Junction. Shortly after the new junction opened in January of that year, a down boat train for Larne Harbour headed by an unidentified U2 class 4-4-0, has just passed under the main line. The viaducts soon weathered and did not stay such a gleaming white colour for long. Charles Friel collection: UFTM L3541/11

Below: The other side of the viaduct is seen in this view, taken on 31st March 1934. The down line to Larne is in the foreground, the siding on the left served Henderson's Mill. On the up main line is a goods for Belfast headed by U2 class No 81 *Carrickfergus Castle*. William Robb: UFTM L4193/9

Above: **Until the junction at Bleach Green was built, all trains for Londonderry had to reverse at Greenisland, which was known as Carrickfergus Junction until 1893. The potential gradients on the direct route, as built in the 1930s, were deemed too arduous for the locomotives being built in the 1840s. When the new line was opened in 1934, the original route was left in place and used for occasional through workings, both passenger and freight, from the Ballymena direction, towards Larne. This section of track became known as the 'back line' and remained in use until the 1960s. In this view of Greenisland taken on 13th May 1950, WT class No 51 is leaving the station with a train for Belfast, as one of the NCC's 1930s railcars arrives at the other side of the island platform on a stopping service from York Road.**
H C Casserley

Centre: **WT No 6 speeds through Mount between Greenisland and Carrickfergus with a passenger train heading for Belfast. This halt opened in 1925 and closed in 1930. It re-opened in 1946 to serve a newly built Courtauld's factory. A siding from the Larne line led to an extensive internal railway system operated by two Peckett-built saddle tanks named *Wilfrid* and *Patricia*. The siding closed in 1967 and the halt five years later.** UFTM L4197/6

Left: **Carrickfergus station was rebuilt when the line was extended to Larne Harbour in 1862 and again enlarged in the 1890s. Like the one at Greenisland, this had three platforms. Most trains stopped at Carrickfergus and some local services terminated here. Exceptions were the boat trains which ran non-stop from Belfast to Larne. A WT tank pauses at Carrickfergus' up platform with a train for Belfast.**
UFTM L4197/8

Top: **Eden was one of a number of new halts opened between Greenisland and Whitehead by the NCC in 1925. The others were Mount (see previous page), Clipperstown, Barn and Downshire Park. From Carrickfergus to Whitehead the line, which stays close to the coast, was doubled in 1929, another example of the investment which the LMS put into its Ulster subsidiary. Eden was closed on 9th May 1977. Of the four new halts opened in 1925, only Clipperstown and Downshire Park, renamed Downshire in 1979, are still in the timetable.** Stations UK No 5811: UFTM L4196/6

Centre: **U2 class 4-4-0 No 80 *Dunseverick Castle* trundles through Downshire Park Halt towards Whitehead with a train of empty wagons.** Reg Ludgate collection: UFTM LUD2537

Bottom: **Railways which skirt the sea are picturesque for travellers but often present problems for those who have to operate them. As mentioned above the section from Carrickfergus to Whitehead was doubled by the LMS. Before the doubling there was a passing place, called Briggs Loop, between Whitehead and Kilroot, the only intermediate station on the stretch from Carrickfergus to Whitehead. Though the incident depicted dates from MR rather than LMS times, it does illustrate the potential hazards of lines like this which hug the coast. On 10th February 1910, just beyond Briggs Loop, the 6.25pm boat train to Larne was derailed by a landslide at a place known as McCann's cutting. The train, which consisted of three passenger carriages, two mail vans and a guard's brake, was derailed. Though two carriages and some of the passengers ended up in the sea, fortunately there were no serious injuries. This view shows the train engine, B class 4-4-0 compound No 62, being prepared to be hauled back on the rails by two engines which had come up from Larne to assist. The rescue operation was completed incredibly quickly and the Stranraer boat which had been held at Larne, was able to depart only a couple of hours behind schedule. It is impossible to imagine the line being reopened so quickly today or the boat being held for delayed rail passengers! This picture is one of a sequence which appeared in the *Daily Mirror*.** UFTM L4196/5.

WHITEHEAD

Above: **The first station at Whitehead in the 1860s consisted of one platform, with an old carriage in use as a waiting room. A new station, still with one platform,** opened on 1st June 1877. A second platform, a passing loop and full signalling were added in 1894. Further improvements were made in 1904 including the erection of a two road engine shed, a goods shed, sidings and a turntable. Whitehead was by now popular with better off commuters and excursionists. The latter were catered for by a new excursion station which opened just off the main line in the Larne direction, on 10th July 1907. The excursion station is now the main base of the Railway Preservation Society of Ireland. In December 1925 the LMS board approved the doubling of the line from Carrickfergus, aided by a 75% grant towards the cost of labour provided by the Northern Ireland government. The work was completed and the new line opened on 6th October 1929. This view, looking towards Belfast, shows the station in the early years of the twentieth century. W A Green: UFTM WAG 757

Left: **No 61 County Antrim passes through Whitehead with goods train travelling towards Larne. Originally built by Beyer Peacock in October 1897 as a B class compound, it was rebuilt in 1932 when it lost its compounding but gained a superheated Belpaire boiler and a name. Withdrawn in 1946, the locomotive is seen here in its post-1932 condition.** UFTM L3535/2

LARNE

Above: **A view of Larne Town station showing the engine shed, goods shed, lamp hut, water tower, platforms and signal cabin. The narrow gauge line to Ballymena ran parallel to the broad gauge line to Belfast at the far end of the station. Broad and narrow gauge drivers were warned not to race each other on this stretch! The rake of narrow gauge carriages in the picture dates the photograph to before 1933 when the narrow gauge passenger service ended.**
W A Green: UFTM WAG527

Right: **In 1964 a travelling circus was moved around Ireland for the last time by rail. The stock of the train provided for the Bertram Mills circus is shunted at Larne Town by WT class tank No 5. It is sobering to reflect that as late as the mid-1960s rail could compete with road for work such as this, but depressing to note that this was also the year that the UTA abandoned rail freight services in Northern Ireland.**
Charles Friel collection: UFTM L4197/5

BROAD GAUGE LOCOMOTIVES

The B&B commenced services in 1848 with eleven engines. Five were supplied by both Bury, Curtis & Kennedy and by Sharp Brothers. The other was bought second hand. This was the ex-Ulster Railway engine *Spitfire*, regauged from 6ft 2in to 5ft 3in and renamed *Hawk*. As the train service increased, it was found that the locomotives were not capable of hauling the loads required, so six new engines were purchased from Sharp Stewart in 1856. Four of these little 2-4-0s were still in service in 1924 although by then, few original parts remained. By the end of 1861 the BNCR had 34 locomotives. Most engines were supplied by Sharp Stewart until the late 1870s when BNCR allegiances changed to the other Manchester firm of Beyer Peacock. For the next 20 years, all new engines came from Beyer Peacock. Bowman Malcolm's passion for compounding meant that from 1890 all new engines were two-cylinder Worsdell von Borries compounds, unusually fitted with Walschaerts valve gear. This brief survey looks at the changing shape of the BNCR/NCC steam fleet from the late nineteenth century until the last new locomotives were delivered after the Second World War.

Below: **Fireman, driver and guard on the footplate of class D loco No 50 *Jubilee* at Portrush.** J H Houston. UFTM M6605

Above: **Bowman Malcolm joined the BNCR Locomotive Department in 1870 aged 16. He became Locomotive Superintendent when he was only 22. An exceptionally capable engineer, even though he had no formal training, he became famous throughout the railway world for his compound locomotive designs. When Wise retired in 1906, Malcolm became head of civil engineering as well. He retired in September 1922 aged 68 having completed 52 years service and died on 3rd January 1933.** UFTM MS548

Left: **Class D compound passenger locomotive No 55 *Parkmount* was built by Beyer Peacock in June 1895. Named after the estate of one of the directors, it began life as a 2-4-0 but within two years was rebuilt as a 4-4-0. Built as a compound, it remained so until its withdrawal in September 1944, making it the longest surviving broad gauge compound. This engine worked mainly on the Derry Central Line in the 1930s.** UFTM L3476/5

Top: **Class L 0-6-0 goods engine No 18 was built in June 1857 by Sharp Stewart. It was rebuilt in 1908. This locomotive had a long working life starting with the Belfast & Ballymena Railway and lasting into LMS ownership, not being withdrawn until 1925. It still retains its original chimney in this photo. The surveyor's level, wheel barrows and other paraphernalia in the foreground indicate that on this occasion No 18 was assisting in the course of some engineering works.** UFTM L4192/11

Centre: **Class F 2-4-0 locomotive No 45, with an ancient four-wheeled passenger carriage, is seen at Portrush about 1900. This inside-framed engine was built by Beyer Peacock at a cost of £2120 in 1880. It was rebuilt with larger cylinders in 1899 and overhauled again in 1912. There were three locos in this class, numbered 23, 45 and 46. Nos 45 and 46 were withdrawn in 1938, No 23 survived even longer than her two sisters, lasting until 1942.**
Charles Friel collection: UFTM L4192/10

Below: **Another very long lived BNCR design was this G class 2-4-0 No 10 which was built by Sharp Stewart in 1876. It was rebuilt as a G1 class in 1910 and remained in service until 1931.**
J H Houston collection: UFTM MS500/57

Left: **Class B3 4-4-0 tender locomotive No 60 *County Donegal* is seen at York Road in August 1938 with a North Atlantic brake coach in the background. Built as a B class compound by Beyer Peacock in 1897, its rebuild as a simple took place in 1932, in which form it lasted until October 1946.** J H Houston: UFTM MS562

Centre: **Class A 4-4-0 tender locomotive No 9 was built in December 1904 at York Road and renumbered 69 in September 1925. It was rebuilt to class A1 in June 1933 with a standard LMS G6 type boiler and named *Slieve Bane*. The loco was finally withdrawn in August 1954. This view, which was taken in about 1940, shows the large gap between the framing and the boiler which distinguished many of the NCC 4-4-0s.** J H Houston: UFTM MS592

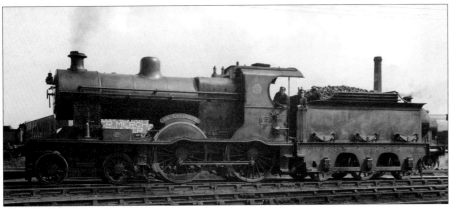

Below: **Class A No 17, built at York Road in January 1907 as a compound, was re-numbered 58 in June 1927. This pre-1923 photograph at Belfast, shows it in its original condition. Following a rebuild to class A1 in February 1934, as a two-cylinder simple with a superheated Belpaire boiler, it was not withdrawn until August 1954.** Reg Ludgate collection: UFTM LUD2506

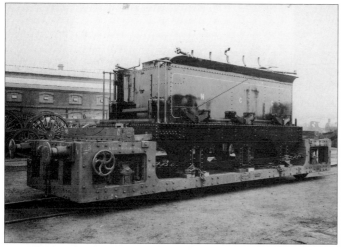

Top: **Following the Midland takeover in 1903 many NCC locomotive were built at Derby. No 70 is seen there after completion in July 1914. Fully painted and lined out, it has been partially dismantled and loaded onto a well wagon for transit to Belfast via the MR's Heysham docks.**
National Railway Museum: DY 10248

Lower left: **No 70's newly built tender, also partially dismantled, is seen on another well wagon, ready for the journey to Belfast. These two photographs were taken at Derby on 13th July 1914.**
National Railway Museum: DY 10245

Lower right: **This was the finished product after reassembly at York Road. U class No 70 was rebuilt to class U2 in 1924, when it was given an LMS G7 type boiler. It was withdrawn in January 1956.** UFTM L3476/9

Above: **Even after the takeover, outside builders continued to be used by the NCC. The now preserved No 74 *Dunluce Castle* was one of seven engines of this type built by the North British Locomotive Company in Glasgow in 1924. On account of where they were built they were known to the men as 'Scotch' engines.**
Reg Ludgate collection: UFTM LUD2541.

Centre: **Class V 0-6-0 superheated goods locomotive No13, built at Derby in February 1923, was to become the last NCC locomotive of this wheel arrangement to remain in service. Her boiler, motion and cylinders were interchangeable with the two U class locos built the previous year. No 13 had 19 x 24 inch cylinders and the standard NCC goods engine driving wheel diameter of 5ft 2in, which permitted brisk running. During her first ten years No 13 was often based at Cookstown Junction. By 1935 her firebox was in a bad state and she did not run at all for two years. After repair she is seen here in January 1939, fitted with a snowplough. Rebuilt as a class V1 in February 1953, No 13 was finally withdrawn by the UTA in 1964.**
J H Houston: UFTM MS578

Left: **The NCC had relatively few tank engines until the arrival of the WT class in the 1940s. Class J 2-4-0 No 49 was built by Beyer Peacock in March 1883 as a side tank and rebuilt in 1891 as a saddle tank. In this view, taken at Larne shed, the fireman is Billy Bell who later became a driver at Draperstown and finally shed foreman at York Road.**
J H Houston collection: UFTM L3147/6

THE MOGULS

Top: **A works photograph of W class 2-6-0 No 90 on temporary 5ft 3in gauge track at Derby works. The locomotive's tender held 2,500 gallons of water and 5 tons of coal.** UFTM archive

NCC services were revolutionised with the appearance of the first of the Derby designed W class 2-6-0s in 1933. Not a standard LMS design, their closest British relatives were probably the Fowler designed 2-6-4 tanks first introduced in 1927. They made use of many standard LMS components including their cylinders, frames and motion. Their boilers were a modified version of the LMS G8A type joined to a shorter and wider firebox, which the more generous dimensions of the Irish

5ft 3in gauge, permitted. They had 6ft driving wheels, larger than those of the LMS tanks, yet smaller pony truck wheels. Though much of the detailed design work on the 2-6-0s was undertaken in Belfast under the supervision of Hugh Stewart, the NCC Locomotive Engineer, their design is notionally acredited to the LMS' Chief Mechanical Engineer, William, later Sir William, Stanier. He had only recently taken up office and though his first design for the LMS had been a small class of 2-6-0s, many of the

characteristics of the NCC 2-6-0s are much more typical of the Midland tradition at Derby than Stanier's later work for the LMS.

Bottom: **No 97 *Earl of Ulster* is seen at York Road shortly after it was built in July 1935.** UFTM L3602/10

Above: The last six Moguls delivered between 1938 and 1942 were supplied with larger capacity tenders which could carry 3500 gallons of water and seven tons of coal. These were similar to tenders being built for new LMS locos in Britain at the time. No 102, is seen at York Road with the larger tender, not long after it entered service in the Spring of 1940.
J H Houston: UFTM MS591

Above: No 91 *The Bush*, along with Nos 90, 92 and 93 were built at Derby, the rest of the 15 strong class were assembled at York Road works using parts supplied by Derby. The original design of tender was similar to that paired with the Midland Railway 2P 4-4-0s in Britain. J H Houston: UFTM MS558

Below: No 98 was named *King Edward VIII* when it entered service in 1937 even though the King had abdicated on 10th December 1936. It was also one of two Moguls, the other being No 95 *The Braid*, which were fitted with LMS-Caledonian Railway hooters, instead of conventional whistles. J H Houston: UFTM MS554

JINTIES

In 1944, to assist with the heavy traffic which the Second World War had brought to the NCC system, two of the LMS' Fowler-designed standard shunting tanks, commonly known as Jinties, were regauged and sent over to Ireland. LMS No 7456, built by Bagnall in 1926, and No 7553, built by Hunslet in 1920, became NCC Y class Nos 18 and 19, respectively. They were initially used on local trains but were mostly employed shunting around York Road and on the dock lines in Belfast.

Right: **No 18 is seen at York Road on 17th April 1948.** H C Casserley: UFTM L3542/5

Below right: **No 18 is about to be craned aboard ship at Heysham for the journey across the Irish Sea.**

Below left: **The loco is reunited with its wheels on arrival in Belfast in 1944.** Both Charles Friel collection: UFTM L4192/13 & 14

Opposite page: **Towards the end of the war, the NCC were desperately behind with locomotive maintenance and called on the assistance of Harland & Wolff. Nine Moguls were taken across to the shipyard on a floating crane for complete overhaul. Afterwards they were tested on the Bangor branch of the BCDR before being returned to their home system via the Belfast Central line and the GNR branch from Lisburn to Antrim. Here, No 104 and her tender are eased across for repair.**

Right: **The floating crane is manœuvered to the quayside at Harland & Wolff by one of the two *Empire* class sea-going tugs which came to Belfast at the end of the war. One of the diesel locomotives built by the firm for the NCC can be observed on the deck of the crane. It was either going across for repair or to shunt the locomotives into the repair shop.** Both Charles Friel collection: UFTM L4194/9 & 10

Above: **No 96 *Silver Jubilee* is nearing completion of her overhaul at Harland's on 18th December 1944.** Harland & Wolff collection: UFTM HW5066

THE JEEPS

This page, above and left: **In 1946, the first four of a batch of 18 2-6-4 tanks were built at Derby for the NCC. The arrival of the WT class tanks completed the modernisation of the NCC steam fleet which the LMS had begun in the 1930s with the W class 2-6-0s. Essentially a tank engine variant of the Moguls, the WT's cylinders, coupling rods, valve gear and boiler were also features of the Fowler 2-6-4 tanks, on which the Moguls were based. Modifications in line with the latest LMS practice included a self cleaning smoke box, rocking grate, outside steam pipes to the cylinders, a comfortable cab with side windows and the coal bunker designed to allow clear vision when the engine was running backwards. Their 6ft driving wheels gave them a good turn of speed and their ability to tackle all types of traffic so impressed William McCullough, night foreman at York Road, that he gave them the nickname 'Jeeps', by which they were often subsequently known. The transport of these large engines to Belfast was difficult. After final assembly each loco was partially dismantled, loaded onto ten wagons and delivered to Heysham.**

The first four, Nos 5 to 8, were brought to Belfast on the LMS cargo ship *Slieve Bloom*. On arrival each was lowered onto two sets of driving wheels for the short journey along the tightly curved harbour lines to York Road, where reassembly was effected.
Both J H Houston: UFTM L4197/1 & 2

Above: No 6, the locomotive shown being landed in the photographs on the previous page, poses for the camera at York Road. No 5 was actually the first one put to work, on 8th August 1946. The livery of the new locomotives was LMS black with straw lining and maroon edging.
Reg Ludgate collection: UFTM LUD2540

Below: The first four Jeeps in steam outside York Road shed when new in 1946. It was suggested at this time that the entire system could be worked by the new engines and that the existing Moguls should be rebuilt as tanks to minimise the use of turntables.
Belfast Telegraph: UFTM L4197/4

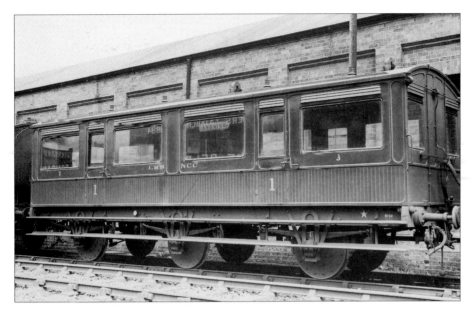

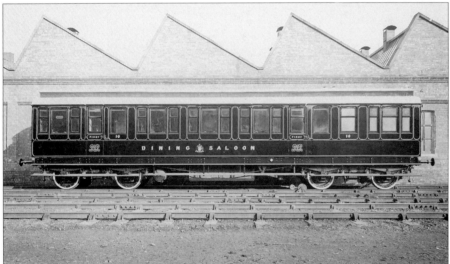

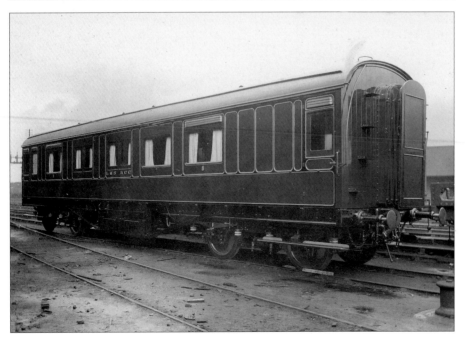

CARRIAGES

Most carriages built for the NCC had similar characteristics to the MR or LMS vehicles of the time. These high waist vehicles had wooden framing and panelling with full beading on the outside. The elliptical roof was of wood covered with canvas, painted and fitted with torpedo ventilators. The ends were tongue and groove match boarding with British standard (scissors type) corridor connections. The carriage was mounted on a 57ft (later 60ft) steel underframe fitted with automatic vacuum brakes, buffers, steam heating and screw link couplings. Most carriages were also fitted with external doors to each compartment. Doors had sliding droplight windows. Lighting was by electricity generated by dynamos and stored in batteries carried beneath the floors.

These handsome carriages were finished in LMS Crimson Lake livery with full lining. They were not quite so attractive inside and were considered cramped when compared with coaches from other Irish companies. Many NCC coaches lasted until the end of steam either as locomotive hauled stock or rebuilt as railcar units. Passenger carriage stock consisted of around 180 broad gauge vehicles. The most numerous types were the class J11, nine-compartment non-corridor Thirds and class J6, eight-compartment corridor Thirds.

Top: **Class Z2 six-wheeled First Class Saloon carriage No 3 was built in 1888. It had seating for 30 in two compartments and weighed 13 tons.** Charles Friel collection: UFTM L4192/15

Centre: **The BNCR's first dining car seen here, was class B1 No 10 built in 1899. In 1902 a menu from the dining car on the noon express to Portrush included the choice for luncheon of lobster, cold veal and ox tongue, pressed beef, chicken and ham, pigeon and ham pie, roast lamb and mint sauce, at a cost of two shillings (ten pence).** R Welch: UFTM L3148/5

Bottom: **NCC class A1 carriage No 8 was built in 1894 for the BNCR and rebuilt as a Royal Saloon in 1924. It was also used to convey directors and other dignatories around the system.** UFTM L3149/3

Above: **The interior of the First Class Dining Saloon No 8. This vehicle had two compartments, one with up to 16 seats for diners, the other with ten easy chairs. It was still in use in the mid-1960s having been renumbered 162 by the UTA in 1959.**
UFTM L3724/7

Right from top: **NCC centre corridor Third Class carriage No 246 under construction in November 1925 at the York Road workshops. This class J4 carriage seated 80 people and had a toilet at each end.**
UFTM L3148/11

NCC class J7 non-corridor Third No 276 was photographed following its construction at the LMS works at Wolverton on 19th June 1933. Seating in this high capacity vehicle, which could accommodate 120 passengers, was six abreast. This carriage was rebuilt by the UTA as Multi-Purpose Diesel Railcar No 52.
National Railway Museum: W318

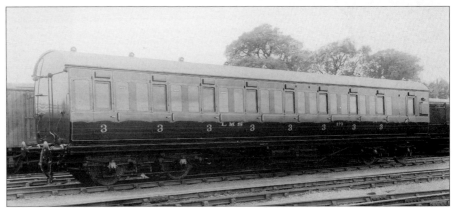

**Class K2 non-corridor Brake Third carriage No 273 was also recorded at Wolverton on its completion in June 1933.
It had look out duckets at one end for the guard and was later rebuilt by the UTA as railcar trailer No 539.**
National Railway Museum: W319

Wolverton built, class H2 non-corridor Tri-composite carriage No 280 was used on steam services into the 1950s, when like many similar vehicles, it was given a new lease of life, being rebuilt as UTA Multi Purpose Diesel railcar No 46.
National Railway Museum: W320

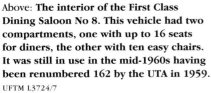

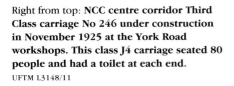

Top, left and below: **Following the building of the viaducts at Bleach Green, the NCC exploited the faster timings possible by introducing a new named train on the Belfast to Portrush route, 'The North Atlantic Express'. Five new and very attractive carriages were built for use on this service and in time these coaches became known as the North Atlantics. The set consisted of a Brake Third, two Thirds, a Tri-composite and Buffet Car No 90, featured here. This vehicle had a cocktail bar and seating for 26 people on chromium plated chairs. The walls were finished in polished mahogany, there was blue linoleum and rugs on the floor. The North Atlantics, with their distinctive deep windows were among the most attractive vehicles to run on the railways of Ireland in the age of steam. In its crimson lake livery hauled by a gleaming Mogul, the train must have been an impressive sight as was its performance. 'The North Atlantic Express' had a start-to-stop booking of 60mph between Ballymena and Belfast, making it the fastest train in Ireland at the time.** Interior view,
J H Houston collection: UFTM L3148/4;
Photo and drawing both UFTM archive.

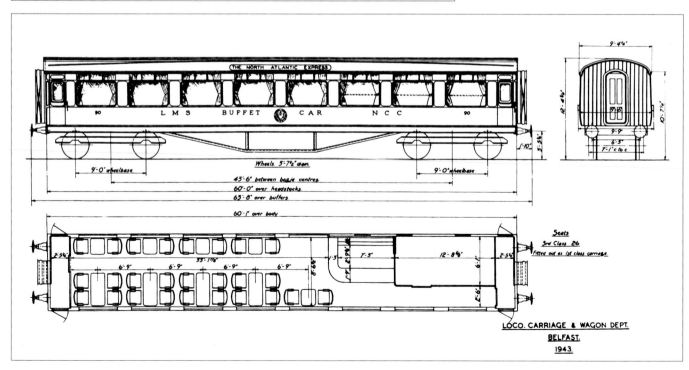

Top: **W class 2-6-0 No 103 *Thomas Somerset* arrives at York Road in the early UTA era, with an express from Londonderry which includes several North Atlantic coaches in its formation.**
Reg Ludgate collection: UFTM LUD2535

Above: **NCC carriage design persisted into the UTA era. Buffet car No 87, reputedly the only rail passenger vehicle built at the UTA's Dunmurry workshops, though some NCC design vacuum braked 'brown' vans were also built there, is seen in the unlikely setting of Donegall Square, in the centre of Belfast. The 60 ft long carriage** was on its way on a low loader hauled from Dunmurry to York Road by a UTA Scammell truck. One of the last passenger coaches to be built in Northern Ireland, when it was withdrawn by Northern Ireland Railways in 1972, No 87 was secured for preservation by the Railway Preservation Society of Ireland. UFTM L4103/7

THE NARROW GAUGE LINES

BALLYMENA, CUSHENDALL & RED BAY RAILWAY

In this part of the book we will explore the narrow gauge lines which the LMS inherited in 1923. The Ballymena, Cushendall & Red Bay Railway was the first narrow gauge line in Ireland to be built with parliamentary authorisation. The slightly earlier and nearby Glenariff line, Ireland's first 3ft gauge railway, was built entirely on private land and thus did not require legislation. The BC&RB was originally promoted as a mineral railway to tap iron ore deposits in the hills and glens of north-east Antrim. The line was opened from Ballymena to Cargan in 1875 and reached its terminus, Retreat, in the middle of nowhere, high above Cushendall, the following year. The railway never did reach Cushendall or Red Bay due to the impossible gradients that would have been required to get it down to sea level. A depression in the iron ore trade led to a decline in traffic and the company was taken over by the BNCR in 1884. The new owners introduced a passenger service for the first time, between Ballymena and Parkmore, the final section from Parkmore to Retreat never carried passenger trains. The BNCR saw the potential of the line to bring tourists to Glenariff Glen. Paths, refreshment facilities and a dark room for photographers were built and passengers were taken from Parkmore to the Glen in road vehicles. Road competition led to the withdrawal of passenger trains in 1930 and by June 1940 the last part of the line open for goods traffic, from Ballymena to a creamery at Rathkenny, finally closed.

Photographs on the opposite page:

Top: **Saddle tank No 60 poses for the camera at Ballymena with two of the carriages built by the BNCR for the introduction of passenger services on the line to Parkmore.** J H Houston collection: UFTM MS500/26

Bottom: **0-4-2 saddle tank No 101 at Parkmore about 1910. At 1,000 ft above sea level this was the highest railway station in Ireland. This locomotive was originally No 1, then renumbered 60, before becoming finally No 101. The station buildings at Cross Roads, Cargan, Parkmore and Retreat were maliciously destroyed by fire on 25th March 1921. The broad gauge signal cabins at Killagan and Dunloy were also burned down in the civil unrest of those years. The station at Parkmore was subsequently rebuilt. Because of its remote location much of the station building and the water tower to the left of the picture are still extant though they have not seen a train since 1930.** Rev W G Davis: UFTM L4107/6

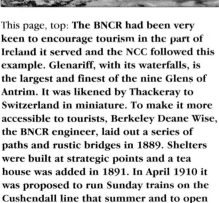

This page, top: **The BNCR had been very keen to encourage tourism in the part of Ireland it served and the NCC followed this example. Glenariff, with its waterfalls, is the largest and finest of the nine Glens of Antrim. It was likened by Thackeray to Switzerland in miniature. To make it more accessible to tourists, Berkeley Deane Wise, the BNCR engineer, laid out a series of paths and rustic bridges in 1889. Shelters were built at strategic points and a tea house was added in 1891. In April 1910 it was proposed to run Sunday trains on the Cushendall line that summer and to open** the glen. The landlord, Robert Hassard, objected but later changed his mind and the trains ran. In 1929, there were 39,320 visitors each paying 6d (2½p) to visit the glen bringing in £983 of which £750 was profit. There were over half a million visitors between 1923 and 1938. The glen was closed during the war and reopened in the summer of 1946 when the admission charge raised to 1 shilling (5p).
W A Green: UFTM WAG 1509

Lower left: **In 1930 Glenariff Glen was finally purchased by the NCC and it was decided that admittance to the glen to those holding NCC rail or road tickets would be free, while others would be charged.** W A Green: UFTM WAG 1503

Lower right: **In 1938 a woman died when she fell from the path at Ess-na-Larach waterfall. In recent years the paths and bridges through the glen have been restored to their former glory.**
W A Green: UFTM WAG 1505B

BALLYMENA & LARNE RAILWAY

Though promoted to exploit Antrim's mineral resources, the B&L carried passengers from the outset. The first section from Larne to Ballyclare was opened in September 1877 and in August the following year the line from Ballyboley, the junction for the branch to Ballyclare, to Harryville on the outskirts of Ballymena, was opened. The line was extended into the BNCR station at Ballymena in 1880. Here it made an end-on junction with the BC&RB line. The Ballyclare branch was extended 1½ miles to Doagh in 1884. After several years of financial uncertainty, the B&L was absorbed by the BNCR in 1889. The first three engines on the line were an 0-6-0 tank and two 2-4-0 tanks, the latter very similar to those supplied by Beyer Peacock to the Isle of Man Railway. The next engine was a unique 2-6-0 saddle tank built in 1880. Another 0-6-0 tank supplied in 1883 completed the fleet. New carriages were supplied in 1928 for the boat trains from Ballymena to Larne, one of the fastest narrow gauge services in Ireland, covering the 25 miles in one hour. These carriages brought main line standards of comfort to the narrow gauge, offering steam heating, electric lighting, lavatories and corridor connections. They had only been in use for five years when passenger services between Ballymena and Larne were withdrawn during the railway strike of 1933. Passenger services had ended between Ballyclare and Doagh in October 1930 and in 1933 that section closed completely. Ballymena to Ballyboley Junction was closed in June 1940, leaving the goods only Ballyclare to Larne line open. This final part of the erstwhile B&L was eventually closed by the UTA in July 1950.

Left: **2-4-0 tank No 4 at Larne shortly after the opening of the line. The carriage closest to the engine is No 5 and the last coach is a First Class Saloon which was lent to the Londonderry & Lough Swilly Railway in 1903 to convey Edward VII between Buncrana and Derry.** R Seggons: UFTM L4124/5

Below: **The most powerful locomotive on the line was this 2-6-0 saddle tank, seen beside the narrow gauge signal cabin at Larne. Known as 'The Bruiser', it was the only engine of this type ever to run on an Irish narrow gauge railway. Built by Beyer Peacock in 1880 at a cost of £1700 and numbered 5 by the B&L, it was first renumbered 68 by the BNCR and then 109 in January 1897. It was rebuilt in 1899 and withdrawn in May 1934.** UFTM L3148/9

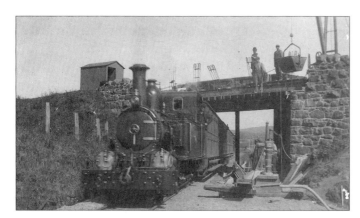

Above: **One of the 2-4-0 tank locomotives with a passenger train passing through a bridge which is either under construction or reconstruction. In this view which dates from around 1910, the temporary water supply for the bridge builders in the foreground, may be noted**. UFTM L4193/14

Above: **4-4-2 tank loco No 113 takes water at Ballyboley Junction cabin, on its way back from bringing a coal train to the paper mill at Ballyclare. In 1945 when this photo was taken the main line beyond Ballyboley to Ballymena had been closed and the traffic generated by the paper mill had become the line's only source of income.** Reg Ludgate collection: UFTM LUD2533

Right: **Bowman Malcolm's passion for compounding extended to the BNCR narrow gauge locomotives built under his stewardship. S class 2-4-2 tank No 110, seen here at Ballymena, was built in 1892 by Beyer Peacock. Originally numbered 69, it was renumbered in 1897. In 1931 this engine was radically rebuilt emerging from York Road works as a 2-4-4, the only locomotive of this wheel arrangement ever to run in Ireland. Though on paper a powerful locomotive, the rebuilt No 110 did not seem to be used very much after its transformation.** UFTM L3148/8

Lower left: **2-4-0 tank No 105 inside Larne shed about 1925. By this time only running repairs were carried out at Larne, for heavy overhauls locomotives were transferred to York Road. This engine was sold to the Castlederg & Victoria Bridge Tramway in 1928.**
UFTM L3542/4

Lower right: **Brake van No 4251, brings up the rear of a short Larne to Ballyclare coal train in 1945. This picture clearly shows the centre coupling, side safety chains, vacuum and steam heating pipes on the vans.** J H Houston collection: UFTM L4124/1

Top: **0-6-0 tank No.106 on transporter wagon No 3045 at York Road works about 1924. This was one of the wagons used to take narrow gauge stock to Belfast for repair. No 106 was built by Beyer Peacock at a cost of £1,560. It was rebuilt in January 1897, again in 1908 and withdrawn in June 1933. In this view it retains its original safety valves, the other two members of the class were fitted with Ross 'Pop' valves.** Reg Ludgate collection: UFTM LUD2532

Centre: **This posed shot at Larne Harbour shows the new carriages supplied for the Larne to Ballymena narrow gauge boat trains in 1928. The train is headed by the former Ballycastle Railway 4-4-2 tank No 113. The leading carriage is Composite First/Third No 350. The other carriages are numbers 352 and 353. These vehicles, built at York Road, were the most luxurious ever to run on the Irish narrow gauge. After passenger services ended on the Antrim narrow gauge lines the coaches saw further service on the County Donegal system.** J H Houston collection: UFTM MS506

Bottom: **One of the narrow gauge boat train carriages, it looks like the composite No 350, on a 5ft 3in gauge transporter wagon at York Road.** UFTM L3148/12

THE BALLYCASTLE RAILWAY

The final narrow gauge line run by the LMS in County Antrim was the Ballycastle Railway which opened on 18th October 1880. It linked Ballymoney, on the BNCR main line, with Ballycastle, a small resort and port some 16 miles distant on the north coast. Built cheaply by a company which never had much money or traffic, loans had to be taken out to complete the line and much of its modest profits had to be used to pay the interest on these. The line was always short of traffic. This decreased markedly after the end of the First World War and consideration was given to winding up the company in 1924. Had that happened it would have been the first 3ft gauge line in Ireland to close. The LMS initially declined to take over the line and services were suspended on 4th April 1924, but eventually agreed to purchase it for £12,500. The line was reopened by the NCC on 11th August 1924. When the Ballymena & Larne section closed to passengers in 1933, the boat train coaches were transferred to the Ballycastle line. The fastest working on the line was the Saturday connection from the noon Belfast to Portrush express. It was timed to cover the 16¼ miles from Ballymoney to Ballycastle in 40 minutes. After the takeover by the NCC, the line was normally worked by one engine in steam. On 1st October 1948 the Ulster Transport Authority was formed and it was expected that certain branch lines would be closed down. The future for the last remaining narrow gauge passenger service in Antrim was bleak. Permanent way maintenance expenditure was kept to a minimum and during the winter of 1948 buses were substituted for trains on Sundays. UTA livery had been applied to the engines and it has often been said that when the paintbrush appears, closure is not far behind. The last train ran on the evening of Sunday 2nd July 1950 decorated with flags and bunting. The three boat train coaches were sold to the CDRJC, arriving at Stranorlar on 20th August 1951.

Right: BR 0-6-0 saddle tank No 2 *Countess of Antrim*, with a mixed train at Ballycastle, was built for the opening of the line in 1880 but was not taken into LMS stock in 1924. The station consisted of a stone and timber structure of considerable pretensions, with a booking office complete with clock tower, arrival and departure platforms and platform awnings. There was a three-road goods yard, a large goods shed and a small wooden engine shed housing one locomotive. UFTM L3284/10

Below: No 2 *Countess of Antrim* and her sister No 1 *Dalriada* were built by Black, Hawthorn & Co. Two further locomotives, Kitson built 4-4-2 tanks, bought by the company in 1908 were retained by the NCC. Third Class carriage seats were not upholstered, which was said to be best suited to the peculiar local requirements of the district. W A Green: UFTM WAG 835

BALLYCASTLE STATION AND NARROW-GAUGE RY. WAG 835

Left: **NCC No 113 at Larne shed. This engine was originally Ballycastle Railway 4-4-2 tank No 3, one of two built by Kitson in 1908. These engines were notorious for slipping, but were otherwise reliable. It was renumbered 113 when the Ballycastle line was taken over by the NCC in 1924 and rebuilt with a lower cab and boiler height to allow it to work on the Ballymena to Larne line where it spent most of the remainder of its life. It was finally withdrawn in July 1946.**
J H Houston: UFTM L4124/7

Centre, left and right: **On Wednesday 12th March 1947, the last train of the day leaving Ballycastle in a snowstorm failed to reach its destination, when 2-4-2 tank No 41 became stuck in a deep drift that blocked the cutting at Ballaney. The crew and 16 passengers spent the night huddled around the stove in the guard's van. All were found safe and well the following day. The line was cleared and normal working was restored on Saturday 16th March.**
Reg Ludgate collection: UFTM LUD2531

Left: **The S class 2-4-2 tanks dominated services on the Ballycastle line for most of the NCC era. No 102, seen here at Ballycastle, was built at York Road in October 1908 and entered service as No 112. It was the first new engine to be fitted with a Ross 'Pop' safety valve. It was renumbered 102 in February 1920 and rebuilt as an S1 class with an extended coal bunker in 1930. Its number was changed again, this time to 42 in November 1939. It was scrapped in 1954 by the UTA.**
J H Houston: UFTM L4124/11

Right: **This was the last of the S class 2-4-2 tanks to be built for the narrow gauge lines in County Antrim. It emerged from York Road works in March 1920 and entered service as No 104. It worked out of Ballymena shed for many years and became No 43 in October 1942. After a heavy overhaul in 1946, it was sent to the Ballycastle line where it worked until its closure in 1950. It was scrapped in 1954.**
J H Houston: UFTM L4124/8

Below: **An aerial view of Ballycastle station taken in the late 1940s. The independent BR company owned 39 open wagons, 15 covered wagons and 5 cattle trucks. Potatoes, sand and gravel, grain, cattle feed and livestock were the main goods carried. The NCC had four camping coaches located here which can be seen in the old cattle dock on the right of the picture.**
J H Houston: UFTM L4124/12

Right: **Ballycastle station looking towards the town around 1930. The viaduct in the foreground carried the railway line over the River Tow. Special late trains were occasionally run in connection with firework displays and military band pageants during the summer season.**
W A Green: UFTM WAG2069

THE PORTSTEWART TRAMWAY

One of the more singular components of the great LMS empire which was formed in 1923, was the Portstewart Tramway. This 3ft gauge line had been Ireland's first roadside steam tramway when it opened in June 1882. It connected the seaside town of Portstewart with its railway station at Cromore, 1¾ miles distant, on the line from Portrush to Coleraine. Trips were made mainly to connect with the arrival and departure of trains at Portstewart station. At first the tramway was modestly successful but it went into receivership in October 1892. It managed to struggle on until June 1897 when creditors petitioned that it be put up for sale. Samuel R Henry, owner of a posting business in the town, was appointed official liquidator. There was only one offer, that of the BNCR, which acquired the tramway for £2100. It then passed with the BNCR to the MR in 1903 and the LMS in 1923. The Great War had a severe effect on many Irish narrow gauge lines. British government control of all Irish railways was enforced from December 1916 until August 1921. During this period wages were raised by around 250% and the cost of working increased accordingly. The slim profits of pre-war days vanished and a combination of high fares and freight charges drove many potential customers into the arms of the emerging motor industry.

By the 1920s the tramway was losing over £700 per year and needed extensive track renewal. The NCC decided to close it down from 31st January 1926 and replace it with a bus service. Thus the Portstewart Tramway holds the melancholy distinction of being the first of Ireland's narrow gauge lines to succumb.

Above: **After closure, locomotives Nos 1 and 2 were put into storage at York Road. In May 1939, No 1 was sent to Kingston-upon-Hull Transport Museum for preservation where it can still be seen today.**
Hull Transport Museum: UFTM L1172/15

Top left: **The Cromie estate, which owned the land around Portstewart, refused to allow the BBC&PJR to bring its line into the town in case it altered the quiet character of the resort. Some 25 years later, the tram was seen as the solution to the inconvenience which this caused.**
W A Green: UFTM WAG 822

Centre left: **A tram leaves the broad gauge station. The double deck carriage at the rear is No 4.** UFTM L4193/10

Left: **Locomotive No 2, built by Kitson in 1883, is seen outside the Post Office at Portstewart. This engine was overhauled in May 1950 and was intended to appear in steam at the 1951 Festival of Britain, though this did not happen. It is now preserved at the Ulster Folk & Transport Museum at Cultra.** UFTM L3538/9

Above: **Locomotive No 3, built by Kitson in 1900 is seen with its luggage van and double deck bogie tramcar at Victoria Terrace Halt in 1925. Looking at this cavalcade it is not hard to sympathise with a poem published in the *Coleraine Chronicle* in November 1923, part of which read; 'O the tram, the Portstewart tram, Heavy and sluggish, slow as a pram.' Arrangements were made by the NCC with S Stuart Henry, the son of the 1897 liquidator, to provide a motor bus service between Portstewart station and the town when the tramway was closed. He was paid £148.5s.4d in 1926 and £100 in 1927. When the NCC withdrew the subsidy in 1932, the service ceased. Ironically in 1927 Portstewart council requested the NCC to make a deviation of the main line to serve the town. Though the government of Northern Ireland offered to provide a grant of 60% of the unskilled labour costs for the work, the NCC declined the proposal. Times had indeed changed since the railway was first built.** UFTM L2087/7

Centre: **Double deck bogie tram No 4, built by Milne of Birkenhead in 1899, is pictured here when nearly new.** UFTM L437/1

Right: **Strolling along the parade at Portstewart towards the tram and its mock Tudor depot on the right, designed by Berkeley Deane Wise.** UFTM L2856/1

THE CDRJC

Following its 1903 takeover of the BNCR, the Midland Railway was keen to extend its interests in Ireland. The MR offered to purchase the Donegal Railway to the alarm of the GNR which saw a powerful competitor moving into its fiefdom. In 1906 an agreement was reached that the GNR and the MR would jointly purchase the narrow gauge Donegal Railway.

The railway was managed by the County Donegal Railways Joint Committee made up of representatives of both the owning companies. Parliament decreed that the MR should be the sole owners of the DR's Londonderry to Strabane line thereby giving it access over its own tracks to the hub of the CDR at Strabane. Two additions were made to the system under the new owners. A branch from Donegal Town to Ballyshannon was completed in 1905 and the nominally independent Strabane & Letterkenny Railway opened in 1909. The CDR was Ireland's

largest 3ft gauge system with 124½ route miles. The MR stake in the CDR passed to the LMS in 1923 and to the British Transport Commission at nationalisation. Progressively managed and an early pioneer of diesel traction, the CDR is widely covered in other publications. These pages serve to remind the reader of the involvement of the LMS in the running of this much loved narrow gauge system. Following the final closure of the CDR's railways in 1959, the company continued to operate buses and lorries until absorbed by CIÉ in 1971.

Photographs on the opposite page:

Top: **The last goods train, hauled by a class 5 2-6-4 tank, is seen leaving Letterkenny for Strabane on the day CDR rail services ended, 31st December 1959.** J Harcourt: UFTM L4194/1

Lower left: **No 11 *Phoenix,* shunting at Strabane in the 1950s, was the CDR's sole diesel locomotive. Converted from an unsuccessful steam tractor supplied to the Clogher Valley Railway in 1928, the loco has been preserved and resides in the rail gallery of the Ulster Folk & Transport Museum at Cultra.**
Charles Friel collection: UFTM L3512/10

Lower right: **Lot No 93, otherwise known as railcar No 19 waiting at Stranorlar to be auctioned off following closure of the system. Nos 19 and 20 were the last railcars put in service in the early 1950s and both were bought by the the Isle of Man Railway in 1961, where they are still to be found.** UFTM L3474/11

Photographs on this page:

Top left: **Class 5A 2-6-4 tank loco No 21 *Ballyshannon* was built by Nasmyth Wilson, works No 958, in 1912. It was renumbered 1 in 1928 and renamed *Alice.* These three locomotives were the last acquired by the CDR. They had larger tanks than the earlier class 5 2-6-4 tanks and were the first narrow gauge engines in these islands with superheaters. This photo was taken at Strabane shortly after the engine was delivered. They remained in service until closure, No 2 *Blanche* has been preserved at Cultra.** UFTM L3313/4

Top right: **Railcar No 17 at Strabane on 16th August 1939. The CDR railcars were built jointly by Walker Brothers of Wigan and the GNR. No 17 was destroyed in a collision near Donegal Town on 28th August 1949.** UFTM L4193/16

Bottom: **Class 5 2-6-4 tank loco No 8 *Foyle* at Londonderry Victoria Road station with a passenger train for Strabane in the early 1950s. This was the line wholly owned by the MR. Services between Strabane and Derry, were operated by the CDR while NCC staff maintained the line and staffed the stations.** J H Price: UFTM L4193/15

THE LNWR CONNECTION

We now turn to the sometimes overlooked Irish entanglements which the LMS inherited through the London & North Western Railway. LNWR activity in Ireland stemmed from its desire to secure or enlarge its share of the cross channel traffic. In 1869 it advanced £30,000 to the Dublin, Wicklow & Wexford Railway in return for shares, to encourage completion of the extension of its line from Enniscorthy to Wexford.

Later, concerned at keeping the Great Western Railway away from the Irish traffic, the LNWR subscribed £100,000 towards the building of the extension of the DW&W line from New Ross to Waterford. The LNWR also paid the Dublin & South Eastern, as the DW&W became in 1907, around £20,000 per year in rebates in connection with cross-channel traffic arrangements. The LNWR had offices at the DSER's Westland

Row station in Dublin. The strategy of keeping the GWR out of Ireland ultimately failed with the development of the ports of Fishguard and Rosslare and their linking railways, in the early twentieth century. The more enduring LNWR legacy, which the LMS inherited, was the railways built by the company in Ireland, in Dublin and to serve the port of Greenore in County Louth.

Above left: **The DN&G line from Dundalk to Greenore crossed the Great Northern Railway's double track main line from Belfast to Dublin on the level at Dundalk Square Crossing, which was between the GNR's Dundalk station and the company's works.**
UFTM L4119/1

Above right: **DN&G 0-6-0 saddle tank No 1** *Macrory* **blowing off steam at Dundalk, before departure for Greenore. Built at Crewe in 1873, works No 1509, No 1 received a new boiler in March 1924. During the Second World War, this engine spent time at Coleraine hauling passenger trains on the Portrush branch.** UFTM L4194/3

THE DUNDALK NEWRY & GREENORE RAILWAY

This railway owed its existence to the LNWR's efforts to increase its share of Irish Sea commerce by developing a port at Greenore to cater for traffic from the north and the midlands. To serve the port a railway opened from Dundalk to Greenore in 1873. A second line, along the shore of Carlingford Lough from Greenore to Newry, was completed in 1876, the service consisting of three mixed trains each way daily. The LMS inherited the DNGR in 1923 but the partition of Ireland in 1921 meant that the DNGR was now partly in Northern Ireland and partly in the Irish Free State. The border adversely effected long established trading patterns. Goods and consignments of livestock were subjected to the delays caused by customs examinations. Passenger steamers ceased to run in 1926 and the railway was losing money from the 1920s onwards. From 1st July 1933, the GNR took over the working of the line from the LMS which helped to reduce losses. In 1948 ownership passed to the British Transport Commission which decided not to subsidise the railway any more, closing it on 31st December 1951. Legal complications arising from the fact that it ran through two different jurisdictions, delayed the final winding up of the concern until July 1957.

Top right: **0-6-0 saddle tank No 2 *Greenore* departing from Greenore with the 2.25pm train for Newry Edward Street on 18th July 1931. The LNWR built a hotel and a golf course at Greenore hoping that it would develop as a tourist resort as well as a port.**
A W Croughton: UFTM L4194/2

Centre right: **A complete LNWR train on Irish soil, DN&G No 3 *Dundalk* with three six-wheeled carriages and a van in 1951. The leading coach is No 2, a composite with gas lighting and steam heating. It was built at Wolverton in 1909 to replace the original stock, which was worn out. This type of vehicle was already obsolete on the LNWR by the time it was built. The carriages, which carried LNWR livery right up to closure, passed to the GNR in 1953. DN&G coach No 1 is now preserved at Cultra.** UFTM L3739/13

Opposite page:

Bottom: **No 5 *Carlingford* with a train of four- and six-wheeled carriages at Dundalk in 1897. The locomotive, later fitted with a cab roof, was built at Crewe in January 1876, works No 1963, and scrapped there in 1928, the first DNGR engine to meet that fate. The Third Class carriage furthest from the engine is a five-compartment four-wheeler.** UFTM L3540/10

Above: **The SS *Galtee More* was one of the LNWR steamers used on the Holyhead to Greenore service. Built by Dennys of** Dumbarton, she was broken up after the withdrawal of the passenger service in 1926. UFTM archive

Top: **On 30th June 1904 locomotive No 6 *Holyhead*, seen here at Newry Edward Street station, headed a special train to Greenore taking harvest workers bound for England. The train was made up of carriages from a variety of companies whose vacuum braking systems were not compatible. The driver left Newry unaware that the brakes would not work on a portion of his train which ran out of control on the descent into Greenore, overrunning the buffers and coming to rest against the wall of a refreshment room. Twenty nine were injured, though none seriously. All were given free food and drink in the company's hotel. When everyone left on the boat** that night they were given a £5 note. It is believed that no claims were ever received by the company. D B McNeill: UFTM L4184/7

Above left: **GNR JT class 2-4-2 tank No 93, now preserved at Cultra, with a DNGR six-wheeled van at Greenore about 1950. These GNR tank engines were regular performers on the DNGR lines after 1933.** UFTM L3540/7

Above right: **No 2 *Greenore*, built at Crewe in 1873 and withdrawn in 1951, is seen at Newry on 9th August 1937.** UFTM L4194/4

NORTH WALL, DUBLIN

Top left: **The LNWR had substantial properties at North Wall in Dublin in support of its shipping interests including a passenger station, offices, a hotel, cattle yard, livery stables and a garage from** which the railway operated a cartage service using motor lorries and horse drawn vehicles. The former LNWR hotel there is now the headquarters of the Civil Engineers Department of Iarnród Éireann. UFTM L4196/8

Top right: **The LNWR North Wall Goods Depot is still open and is now used by Iarnród Éireann as a Container Terminal.**

Vast numbers of Irish cattle travelled via the North Wall to English livestock markets. National Railway Museum: CR C175

Bottom: **The exterior of the LNWR's North Wall station. The closed cab is known as a Brougham or a Growler, the vehicle on the left is a jaunting car.** National Railway Museum: LMS E480

Above and left: **In 1877 the LNWR helped to fund the Great Southern & Western's link line from Kingsbridge to Glasnevin Junction. Trains from Kingsbridge then followed the Midland Great Western's Liffey branch, via West Road and Church Road Junctions, to reach the LNWR's new passenger station, which opened on 2nd September 1877, beside the berth where their steamers tied up on the North Wall. The same year the GNR completed a spur from East Wall Junction to Church Road Junction with financial assistance from the LNWR. These lines gave the LNWR access to the railway systems of the GSWR, GNR and MGWR. The opening of the City of Dublin Junction Railway over the Liffey viaduct in 1891 finally linked Amiens Street to Westland Row connecting the DWWR to the other railways in Dublin and the LNWR's North Wall station. The LNWR advertised that passengers using its vessels could travel to any station in Ireland without the inconvenience of crossing Dublin. Known as the railway with no trains, as the LNWR had no stock of its own in Dublin, the trains serving their station were provided by the other railway companies operating in the city. Regular time-tabled passenger trains to the North Wall had stopped by November 1922.** Both National Railway Museum: CR C176 and LMS E486

AT PEACE AND WAR

In this part of the book we will reflect on some of the innovations introduced on the NCC, mostly in the period following the formation of the LMS.

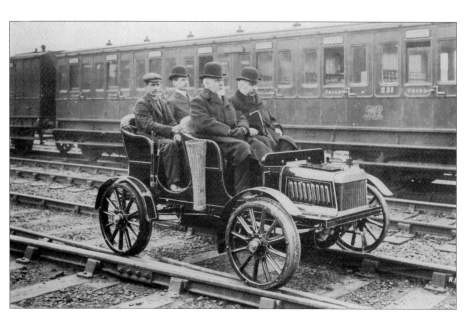

Top: **This early motorised inspection vehicle was purchased from Allday and Onions for the Permanent Way Department in 1905, at a cost of £190. The bowler hatted man in the back is Freeman Wills Crofts, Berkeley Deane Wise's nephew. Crofts, District Engineer at Coleraine and later Assistant Chief Engineer, was the author of some 40 detective novels, which frequently included a railway scene which he often tested out on the NCC. In 1929, he resigned to write full time and in the 1940s had his own BBC Radio series called Inspector French Investigates. Another vehicle from this manufacturer was supplied for the same purpose to the DR in 1907. In 1920 this was rebuilt as a ten seater railcar, the first of the long line of such vehicles used on the CDR.** R Welch: Ulster Museum, W48/01/43.

Below: **Sentinel built railcar No 401 and locomotive No 91 at York Road on 5th August 1930. No 401 had a vertical boiler, a 4 wheel chain-driven power bogie and could seat 55 Third Class passengers. Neither was considered a success and no more such vehicles appeared on the railway.** H C Casserley: UFTM L4194/6

Left: **This LMS Leyland Lion PLSC3 32 seater bus was converted into a railbus by the NCC but retained its road fleet number 42 and its Derby, CH7910, registration plate. A typical daily roster for the Derry based railbus was Derry-Coleraine-Portrush, Portrush-Coleraine-Derry and, after a change of driver there, Derry-Coleraine and then back to Derry.** UFTM L3800/14

RAILCARS

The NCC experimented with railcars throughout the first half of the twentieth century. Two steam railcars numbered 90 and 91 were built in Derby and delivered to Belfast in June 1905 to be used on Belfast to Ballymena stopping trains. Many British railway companies tried similar vehicles at this period and few lasted for any length of time. The locomotive units were scrapped in July 1913 and the bodies rebuilt as coaches, Nos 79 and 80. A 1920 AEC petrol omnibus was converted to run on rails and used between Coleraine and Portrush in early 1924, but was scrapped the following year. Railcar No 1 became the company's first successful modern railcar when introduced in 1933. It was followed by three diesel railcars, for use on local passenger trains. These vehicles survived into the UTA era.

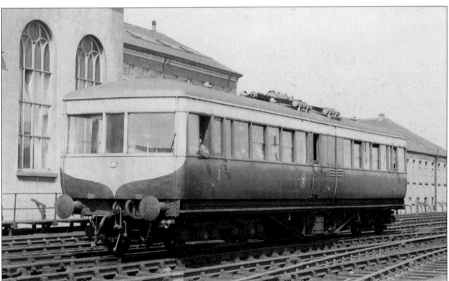

Top: **The first NCC light railcar, No 1 was built in January 1933 at Belfast York Road. Powered by two Leyland petrol engines, it proved to be very satisfactory in service. It had hydraulic transmission in low gear and direct drive in top gear. Subsequent railcars were diesel powered. This view of No 1 in its original condition is believed to have been taken at Jordanstown on the Larne line.** UFTM L3313/2

Centre: **Railcar No1 at Belfast York Road in Ulster Transport Authority livery. No 1 had accommodation for 6 First and 55 Third Class passengers. The original petrol engines were replaced with a pair of diesel engines in 1947.**
Charles Friel collection: UFTM L4194/7

Bottom: **NCC diesel railcar No 2 at Belfast York Road. When it was introduced this railcar normally operated between Belfast, Greenisland, Carrickfergus, Whitehead and Larne. On Saturday afternoons it ran to Ballymena. Railcars Nos 2, 3 and 4 were fitted with turrets above their driving cabs so that they could propel special low roofed trailers. When being operated in this mode their drivers must have had a restricted view of the road ahead. This practice ceased after a trailer being propelled in this way hit a cow and was derailed.** UFTM L3633/1

Right: **Railcar No 4 under construction in York Road workshops on 25th March 1938. It entered service towards the end of that year working mainly between Belfast and Greenisland. It also completed daily runs to Carrickfergus, Larne, Ballymena and Dunloy.** *Belfast Telegraph* collection: UFTM L3354/10

Below: **This photograph of railcar No 4 at York Road in February 1939 was taken by Harold Houston who spent all his working life as an engineer on the NCC. These railcars brought a significant increase in service frequency to suburban stations on the Larne line. The livery is LMS crimson lake, with cream or 'spilt milk' on the upper panels.** J H Houston: UFTM MS582

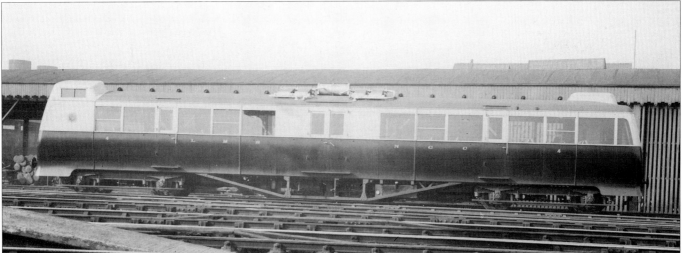

Right: **Railcar No 3 was brought into use in September 1936. It was based at Ballymena for workings to Belfast and was also used on the Larne line as far as Carrickfergus. It is seen here in UTA livery at Whitehead, lying over between duties, in the access road to the Excursion station platforms.** Reg Ludgate collection: UFTM L3366/11

Above: **Railcar trailer No 1 is being propelled out of Kilroot station in the direction of Belfast, past a typical NCC somersault signal, in 1947. Due to the success of the railcars, in July 1933 it was proposed to construct two lightweight** trailers for use with them to meet the need for increased accommodation. Centre corridor trailers each seating 100 passengers were built. They were 62 feet long and at 17½ tons were very light considering their high seating capacity. They were also noticeably lower than normal coaching stock so that the driver, in his turret, could see over them when propelling the trailer.
Reg Ludgate collection: UFTM LUD 2508

DIESEL LOCOMOTIVES

Above: **Harlandic diesel No 17, recorded shunting coaches at Belfast York Road on 5th February 1937, was one of a number of locos built by the famous Belfast ship builders for the NCC at an early stage in the application of diesel traction to railways.** This powerful unit gave excellent service shunting Belfast yard around the clock with a break of 6 hours every Monday for maintenance.
Harland & Wolff collection: UFTM HW6026

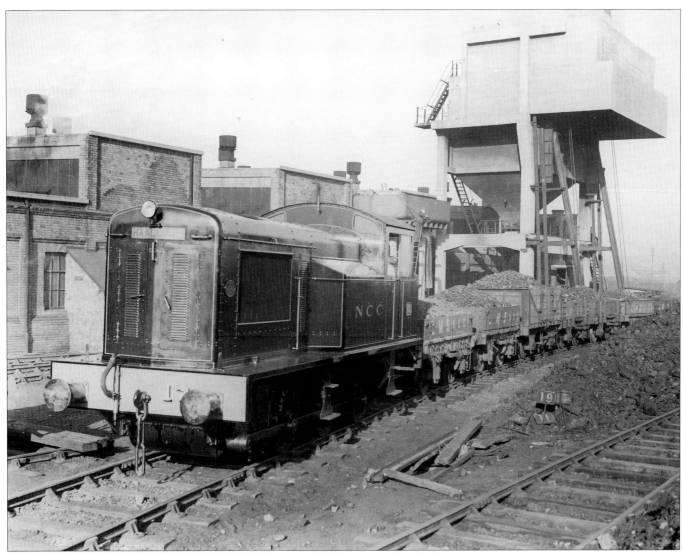

Top: **Harlandic diesel mechanical No 17 with a rake of coal wagons at York Road's coaling tower. This LMS structure was one of only three mechanised coaling plants in Ireland. Wagons of coal were hoisted off the rails, their contents were then tipped into a hopper at the top. Locomotives ran under the tower and had their tenders filled quickly by gravity. This view dates from February 1937 about two years after the coaling plant was built.**
Harland & Wolff collection: UFTM HW6027

Right: **In an effort to diversify their business during the bleak years of the 1930s, Harland & Wolff built a number of diesel locomotives. The NCC became their best customer, buying five. Another of these was 0-4-0 No 20, seen at York Road on 17th September 1945.**
A W Croughton: UFTM L3542/18

LMS No 7057

The British standard gauge diesel shunting loco-motive dates from the 1930s when the LMS works at Derby built a diesel shunter on the frames of an 0-6-0 steam locomotive. Several heavy engineering firms then produced experi-mental designs which were tested and evaluated by the LMS and generally gave satisfactory results. Many different transmissions have been used in shunter design, the most efficient and cost effective combination is an engine driving an electric generator to provide electric power for the traction motors which drive the wheels. These experimental locomotives were supplied by companies such as Drewry, Hunslet, Hudswell Clarke, Armstrong Whitworth, English Electric, Hawthorn Leslie and the Belfast ship-building firm of Harland & Wolff. The latter's contribution was LMS No 7057 which was exported to England, probably the only Irish-built diesel ever to run on the other side of the Irish Sea. This offers a different aspect to the LMS's involvement in Ireland though not a per-manent one. The locomotive was returned to its makers in 1945, whereupon it was re-gauged to 5ft 3in for use on the NCC.

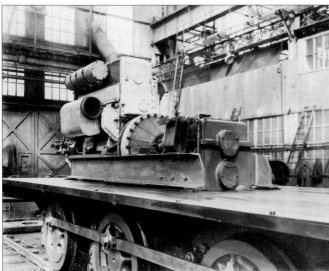

Top: **No 7057 stands completed in the Harland & Wolff workshops on 5th May 1934. The locomotive weighed 27 tons 7 cwt, had a fuel capacity of 105 gallons and a maximum speed of 10 mph.** Harland & Wolff collection: UFTM H&W 3330

Above: **The engine was fitted onto the frames on 6th April 1934 having been run on a test bed two days previously. The engine was a Harlandic TR4 delivering 150 horse power. It had a tractive effort of 11,200lbs. The power was transmitted mechanically to the wheels.** Harland & Wolff collection: UFTM H&W 3310

Right: **In this view No 7057 is standing on a length of adjustable track laid to its 4ft 8½in gauge. Harland-built diesels were also sold to railways in Sudan, Argentina, Canada and New South Wales.** Harland & Wolff collection: UFTM H&W 3336

BLEACH GREEN VIADUCTS AND THE GREENISLAND LOOP LINE

The most important engineering project on the NCC during the LMS period was the building of the Greenisland loop line between Belfast and Antrim. Work started in 1931, was completed in 1934 and was carried out with government assistance as an unemployment relief scheme. The new line from Bleach Green Junction to Monkstown Junction was four miles long and enabled trains to run straight through from Belfast to Antrim without having to run to Greenisland on the Larne line, and then reverse up to Monkstown to regain the main line, as had previously been the case.

At the Belfast end two large reinforced concrete viaducts were built spanning Valentine's Glen. The larger viaduct was 630 feet long with a maximum height of 70 feet and carried the new double track main line on a continuous curve. Trains bound for Larne passed underneath the main line in a burrowing junction before crossing the glen on a separate viaduct. The total cost was £65,000. The viaducts consumed 17,000 cubic yards of concrete and 700 tons of steel reinforcing. This was the last major civil engineering scheme carried out on an Irish railway until the construction of the Dargan bridge over the River Lagan in Belfast in the 1990s. The new route had been considered when the line was being planned in the 1840s, but the steep gradients involved were thought to be beyond the powers of the locomotives of that era. It was mooted again in the 1870s but it was considered that the money would be better spent on fitting automatic vacuum brakes to trains instead.

The notion of the diversion cropped up again in the early 1920s and it was surveyed by Freeman Wills Crofts. In 1933, a young Queen's University graduate named Harden Glendinning was employed to mark out the route again. He found many of the original survey markers put in by Crofts a decade before were still in place, showing the accuracy of his surveys.

Top: **A reinforced concrete bridge for the new up Larne line is under construction on Friday 15th September 1933.**
William Robb: UFTM L4195/7

Centre: **The main line viaduct under construction in 1933 as a passenger train on the new down line to Larne passes underneath. The old down Larne line, on the extreme right of the picture, is being used as a siding for wagons.**
Bryan Boyle collection: UFTM L4195/8

Above: **The temporary platform in the foreground was built, on the main viaduct, for VIPs on the opening day. The left hand line is the down line to Derry, the line under the temporary platform is the up line from Derry.** William Robb: UFTM L4195/9

Above: **A view of the new main line viaduct at Bleach Green during the opening ceremony on Wednesday 17th January 1934. W class Mogul No 90 *Duke of Abercorn*, is in attendance.**
Bryan Boyle collection: UFTM L4195/10

SIGNALLING

Berkeley Deane Wise invented and patented his own train staff system which was later used for working the single track between Ballymena and Retreat and on the Clogher Valley Railway. At each end of the staff were locked pockets containing different coloured metal tablets called train permits, each engraved with the name of the station that they authorised the train to proceed to. Wise's system was safer than the staff and ticket system normally used for single line working but was not widely adopted. In 1899 he equipped the Belfast to Derry, Belfast to Larne and Coleraine to Portrush lines with Manson tablet snatching system apparatus. This was extended to cover the Cookstown and Limavady branches over the next few years.

Top: **One of the Moguls with a high-sided tender passing a somersault signal at Portrush. The black wooden box on the signal post is a platform indicator that displayed a numbered board to the driver. Signal posts were made of best quality pitch pine. The BNCR was the only Irish railway to use somersault semaphore signals. The sand in the foreground has blown up from the beach.** Reg Ludgate: UFTM LUD 2509

Centre left: **Although the BNCR adopted somersault signals from the late 1880s, some conventional lower quadrant semaphore signals, such as those seen in this view of a train leaving Larne Town station, remained in service until replaced eventually by colour lights.** *Belfast Telegraph* collection: UFTM L3331/7

Bottom left: **At Larne Harbour, LMS style upper quadrant signals were erected in 1939. This was the only place in Ireland where upper quadrant signals were used.** Charles Friel collection: UFTM L4195/16

Opposite page:

Bottom: **The Manson Tablet exchange equipment was fitted to engines and erected at the side of the track. It enabled engines to pick up the tablet, which authorised them to proceed into the next section of single track ahead, without stopping or slowing to collect it. The tablet catcher mounted on the cabside could be lowered by the crew to exchange tablets at speed. Locomotive No 51, seen at the north end of Macfin station in 1936, displays the tablet catching apparatus affixed to its cabside. This view also clearly shows the unusual typeface used on NCC cast number plates.** O S Nock: UFTM L4196/1

Above left: **Coleraine station showing the new three aspect colour light signals on 1st December 1938. The pneumatic tyred Leyland Lion rail bus is entering the platform on a working from Ballymena.** *Belfast Telegraph* collection: UFTM L3350/3

Above right: **A close up view of the lineside tablet exchanging apparatus which allowed trains to pass from one section to the next, without slowing down. This equipment which was positioned near a signal cabin, would catch a tablet in a leather pouch from a train leaving one section of track** and exchange it for one for the next section. The upper part of the mechanism caught the tablet being dropped off, the square leather pouch containing the tablet for the next section can be seen on the top left of the picture. Charles Friel collection: UFTM L4196/3

Left: **Carrickfergus signal cabin was built to the standard BNCR design adopted in the 1890s. A detailed drawing and specification of the design by Wise appeared in the April 1893 issue of** *The Railway Engineer*. **The cabins were to be constructed of first quality Belfast brick, the superstructure was made of pitch pine and the roof covered with Bangor blue Welsh slates. The cabin and main station buildings at Carrickfergus were on the up platform which was linked by a subway to an island platform on the down side, which had a loop behind it.** Reg Ludgate collection: UFTM LUD 2510

Below: **An interior view of Carrickfergus signal cabin showing the 40 lever McKenzie & Holland frame which was installed inside.** Charles Friel collection: UFTM L4196/2

THE SECOND WORLD WAR

Below: **The NCC in common with railways in Britain reduced its speeds after the outbreak of war. It withdrew many local services on the Belfast to Derry line, long distance trains making additional stops to compensate. As the war continued, the NCC became very busy with almost every station handling additional military traffic. One remarkable consequence of the war came about in 1943, when the main runway at RAF Ballykelly had to be extended to allow Liberator aircraft to be brought into action against German U-Boats in the Battle of the Atlantic. The only way this could be done was to extend the runway across the NCC main line, between Ballykelly station and Limavady Junction. Special signalling and telephone arrangements were made linking the base's control tower and the railway's signal cabin. This was the only place in these islands, and probably in the world, where a main line railway crossed the runway of an important air base. In this wartime view, probably a posed publicity shot, an RAF Liberator, which is actually parked on the runway, gives the impression of awaiting the passage of an NCC train to Derry.** UFTM L3245/10

Above: **Women were encouraged to go to work during the war. Here women are seen cleaning carriages at York Road station in Belfast. Carriage No 199 (LMS No 11127)** was one of the LMS coaches sent from England in 1942 to replace stock destroyed in the air raids of the previous year. *Belfast Telegraph* collection: UFTM L3350/6

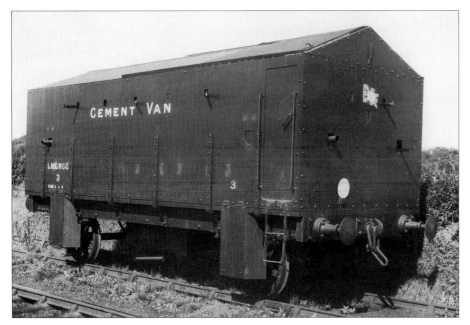

Left and below left: **One of the more bizarre contributions to the war effort was NCC cement wagon No 3, the Northern Counties equivalent to Corporal Jones' butcher's lorry in the Dads Army television comedy series. It was one of three Armoured Rail Trollies manned by the 8th Railway Construction and Operating Company, Royal Engineers, who were based at Whitehead. The vehicles were powered by Leyland engines. The driver kept a lookout by means of a periscope. The forward portion of the roof could be slid back for light and ventilation, the aperture being protected by wire mesh. These photographs were taken on manoeuvres at Antrim in 1941. How the mighty German Wehrmacht would have trembled had it been confronted by this terrible weapon!** Imperial War Museum: H13503 and H13495

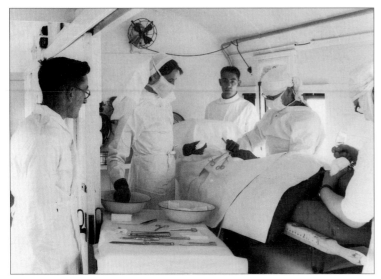

Above and left: **A British Army Ambulance Train was stationed at Whitehead in October 1940. It was stored at the Excursion station platform. The Whitehead train fortunately never saw serious action though it did travel to Londonderry to collect casualties from the *Bismarck* action and bring them back to Belfast. The ward coaches each held 40 patients. The interiors were painted white and had polished linoleum floors. The treatment coach included an operating/dressing theatre, a pharmacy and medical store and a utility room that could be used as an isolation ward or a padded cell. The train and medical staff were accommodated in two coaches containing bunk beds. The kitchen coach could provide meals for four hundred people and was manned by two sets of cooks, one for staff and the other for the patients.** Imperial War Museum: H10391 and H10395

Above: **Following the Japanese attack on Pearl Harbour and the entry into the war of the United States, it became clear that large numbers of American troops would have to be accommodated in the United Kingdom to prepare for the eventual invasion of Europe. Northern Ireland was deemed a suitable location for part of this friendly invasion and a great number of GIs and their equipment were moved to the province. Many of these troops were based in areas served by the NCC. The first American soldiers to arrive in Europe are greeted at Belfast on 26th January 1942 by Mr J W Hutton, the NCC company secretary. The helmets worn by the soldiers in the picture are of the type worn in the Great War rather than the more familiar American Second World War helmets which came later.**
Belfast Telegraph collection: UFTM L4330/4

Right: **At the commencement of hostilities in 1939, a blackout was introduced in Northern Ireland and information on air raid precautions were widely circulated. This is one of the notices issued on these matters by the NCC at this time.**
UFTM archive

London Midland and Scottish Railway Company—Northern Counties Committee.

NOTICE TO PASSENGERS.

AIR RAID PRECAUTIONS.

DURING AN AIR RAID:—

1. Close all windows and ventilators and pull down the blinds as a protection against flying glass.

2. If danger seems imminent, lie on the floor.

3. Never leave the train between stations unless so requested by a Railway Official.

4. Do not touch any outside part of a coach if a gas attack is suspected.

DURING BLACK-OUT HOURS:—

1. KEEP ALL BLINDS DRAWN.

2. KEEP ALL WINDOWS SHUT, except when necessary to lower them to open doors.

3. MAKE CERTAIN the train has STOPPED AT A PLATFORM and that you alight on the PLATFORM side.

4. WHEN LEAVING THIS COMPARTMENT, close windows, lower blinds again and close the door quickly.

A7770—2,000—7/41

Photographs on page 78: **The precautions taken by the NCC had very little effect in the face of the devastating raids on Belfast made by the Luftwaffe in April and May 1941. The city was inadequately defended and the German bombers met little opposition as they concentrated their attack on the city centre, the docks and harbour area and the Harland & Wolff complex. On the night of 15th-16th April York Road station was attacked. The main running lines outside the station received direct hits and offices and stores were destroyed. But worse was yet to come. On the night of 4th-5th May, the Luftwaffe visited Belfast again with even more destructive results for the NCC. The area around York Road station suffered great damage. Most of the remaining office accommodation at the station was destroyed along with the station's overall roof. The station hotel was largely reduced to rubble and extensive damage was done to the works and goods sheds. Twenty passenger coaches were burnt out and over 250 wagons destroyed or seriously damaged. Some of these wagons are seen, opposite top, in the sidings at York Road shortly after the raid. A sense of the devastation caused elsewhere is given in the other picture, where men of the 8th Railway Construction Company Royal Engineers assist with clearing rubble in what remains of the outward goods shed at York Road.**

These raids also caused massive damage at the Harland & Wolff shipyards across the harbour and over 700 civilians were killed in various parts of the city. The death toll would have been even higher had not a large number of its citizens left the city in the months before.
Belfast Telegraph: UFTM L4330/5 & 6

Below: **The damage to York Road's overall roof is apparent in this view of passengers, many of whom are in uniform, pouring out of the 1.45pm train from Larne Harbour, in April 1945.** *Belfast Telegraph*: UFTM L4330/3

Above: **To make up for the loss of so many coaches in the air raids, the LMS sent over a number of old carriages to the NCC. These were put into service as soon as they were regauged. One was LMS No 14102, a non-corridor Third, which came from the erstwhile Manchester, South Junction & Altrincham Railway. Photographed on 6th January 1950, it had still not been repainted. Its NCC number was crudely painted on the door of the end compartment.** UFTM L4103/8

BY LAND, SEA AND AIR

The BNCR was the first railway in Ireland to use mechanically propelled vehicles for passenger road services. On 1st April 1902 it began to operate two Thornycroft 14-seater steam omnibuses on short runs from Greenisland station to Whiteabbey, Seapark and Silverstream. Unfortunately, these buses cut up the roads so badly that they were withdrawn in 1908 and replaced by horse-drawn wagonettes, somewhat similar to those used when these services had started back in the mid-1880s. The NCC did not become a large-scale bus operator until after the passing of the Railway (Road Vehicles) NI Act in 1927.

ROAD SERVICES

Right: **A map showing both the railway and bus services operated by the NCC in 1934. By this time NCC bus services in the counties of Antrim and Derry covered about 565 route miles, practically double that of its railways. The passing of the 1927 Act enabled railway companies in Northern Ireland to run road services under conditions similar to those enjoyed by private operators. The NCC, with the financial resources of the LMS behind it, was able to take full advantage of the legislation. In 1929 it began a vigorous policy to build up a virtual transport monopoly throughout its territory. It was hoped this would lead to substantial savings including the withdrawal of unprofitable passenger services from branch lines. The NCC began to buy out its competitors and by the end of 1934 had taken over the businesses of 17 private operators who had been running buses on its territory.** UFTM L3713/9

Centre right: **In its early days as a road passenger operator, the NCC had been handicapped in that its buses terminated at the kerb side in different parts of Belfast. The opening of a central bus depot at Smithfield on 1st November 1930 ended this inconvenience. The 220ft long depot, photographed here in May 1931, could house 40 buses in its main bay.**
A R Hogg: UFTM L3781/4

Bottom right: **Also in 1931 the company introduced fixed bus stops for the first time. Previously buses had stopped anywhere on request to pick-up or set down passengers. Another innovation was the extension of the validity of season tickets which became interchangeable between road and rail, probably the first time that this facility had been given to season ticket holders in these islands. An Albion Valkyrie bus is seen here at a stop in York Road Belfast, about 1934.**
Bryan Boyle collection: UFTM L3781/6

Photographs on page 80:

Top left: **A maker's photo of one of the BNCR's 1902 Thornycroft steam buses.**
J M Cummings collection: UFTM L4196/9

Top right: **An NCC 31-seater Leyland at Portstewart station. This bus was supplied new to the Belfast Omnibus Company in 1927.** Bryan Boyle collection: UFTM L3780/12

Bottom: **In 1905 the NCC acquired two Thornycroft petrol engined charabancs to operate tours from its Portrush hotel.**
UFTM L1529/5

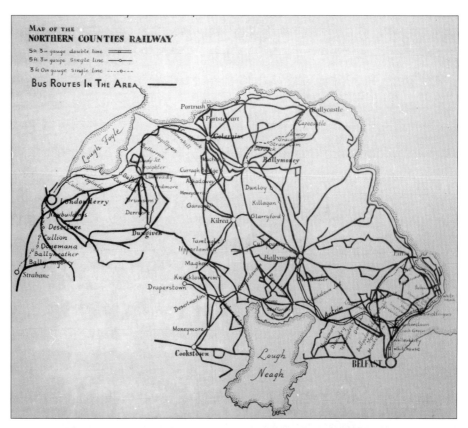

MAP OF THE
NORTHERN COUNTIES RAILWAY

BUS ROUTES IN THE AREA

Top left: **During its last years as a road transport operator, the NCC took steps to standardise its fleet by purchasing mainly Leyland and Albion buses. All its buses were painted in Midland red, the same colour as its railway carriages. They had white roofs and black mudguards and the name 'Northern Counties' was written on the sides of the vehicles. These Leyland Tigers are on an outing from the Laharna Hotel in 1935.** Bryan Boyle collection: UFTM L3781/14

Centre left: **The busiest route operated by the NCC was that between Belfast and Carrickfergus with over 45 workings on weekdays. When the government of Northern Ireland created the Northern Ireland Road Transport Board in 1935 and forced the railways to give up their road services, the NCC was the second largest bus operator in the province owning 131 buses, all of which were single deckers. These seven Albion PH49 Victors were supplied to the NCC in 1933. Their registration numbers were CZ2010-2016 and they had 20 seater Alexander bodies.** Bryan Boyle collection: UFTM L3781/5

Left: **The trade depression of the early 1930s and the unrestricted competition between rail and road for traffic, especially freight, led the Northern Ireland government to seek advice about its transport problems from Sir Felix J C Pole, the recently retired General Manager of the Great Western Railway in England. The substance of his advice formed the basis of the Northern Ireland Road and Rail Act of 1935. Under this Act the operation of all public road services passed to the NIRTB. As well as losing control of their bus services, the railways had to give up their road freight services to the new board. Thus the NCC was no longer able to operate road freight vehicles such as this cattle lorry, photographed at the Balmoral Agricultural Show in the early 1930s.** UFTM L3313/6

NCC HOTELS

Top: **The NCC had hotels at Portush and Larne. The Northern Counties hotel at Portrush had more than 100 bedrooms. The building dated back to the middle of the nineteenth century. It had been built to accommodate tourists visiting the nearby Giant's Causeway, probably Ireland's most famous tourist attraction. The hotel was leased by the BNCR in the 1880s and purchased outright in 1891. Hotel porters met all trains and transport for guests was provided from the station. A new ballroom was added at the turn of the century and an indoor swimming pool was completed in 1935. The hotel was closed in September 1940 and for the rest of the war was used by Campbell College, a school which had been evacuated from Belfast.**
W A Green: UFTM WAG 239

Centre right: **The Laharna Hotel at Larne was the largest tourist hotel in Ireland. It was acquired by the NCC in 1909 around the time that this photo was taken. It was a popular starting point for tours of the Antrim coast.** W A Green: UFTM WAG 542

Below: **The Laharna Hotel catered for tourists wishing to have all in holidays. A typical package included transport to Ulster, daily motor coach excursions, meals and accommodation. This 1920 photo shows Dennis, Ford and Maudslay buses loaded with tourists parked outside the hotel.** UFTM L2148/2

WHITEHEAD & THE GOBBINS

Top: **The NCC not only built hotels to accommodate tourists, the company saw the need to develop attractions to keep visitors interested once they had arrived. The best known example of this was the creation of the walkways and bridges at Glenariff (see page 49). A similar enterprise was undertaken at Whitehead, the spectacular coastal setting of the town can be seen from the above view of a train leaving there for Belfast on 17th July 1932.** *Belfast Telegraph* collection: UFTM L4107/4

Centre: **In August 1902 the BNCR opened an elaborate two mile long coastal path round the great basalt cliffs known as The Gobbins. In its heyday, this was more popular than the Giants Causeway. Designed by Wise, the path incorporated tunnels and spectacular bridges. A BNCR advertisement of the time proclaimed that the cliff path along The Gobbins, 'with its ravines, bore caves and natural aquariums, has no parallel in Europe'. Reached from either Whitehead or Ballycarry stations where jaunting cars met the trains, the path fell into disuse during the Second World War and was closed completely in 1961.** W A Green: UFTM WAG 516

Bottom: **LMS staff at Whitehead pose for the camera in the 1920s. The station nameboard reminds travellers of the delights of the coastal paths developed by the railway.** UFTM L3334/12

SHIPPING SERVICES

Top left: **The development of tourism was
closely linked to another important part
of the railways' activities, that of shipping
services on the Irish Sea. The service from
Larne to Stranraer, promoted then and now
as the short sea route, first opened in 1862
but closed down after fourteen months.
It re-opened in 1872 when an overnight
service between London Euston and Belfast
via Stranraer and Larne was established.
The steamship service was closely
associated with the BNCR. In 1890 the
steamship company which operated on
the route was purchased by a consortium
which included the BNCR, MR and LNWR.
The railway station at Larne Harbour was
beside the steamer berth and connecting
trains ran to and from Belfast and
Londonderry. This photograph shows
BNCR goods wagons and the end of the
platform at Larne Harbour in the early
1880s. The paddle steamer is probably
Princess Beatrice which was launched
by Harland & Wolff at Belfast on 7th
November 1875. It was 235 feet long and
displaced 550 tons.** A R Hogg: UFTM Hogg 138

Centre left: **In 1904 the Midland Railway
opened its own harbour at Heysham
from which it started a service to Belfast.
This carried passengers, mails, parcels,
merchandise and livestock. In 1928 the
LMS decided to withdraw its steamers
from Fleetwood, which was just south of
Heysham, and concentrate their activities
on the Belfast to Heysham route.
The LMS occupied two berths on Donegall
Quay in Belfast and two adjoining transit
sheds belonging to Belfast Harbour
Commissioners. The railway company
owned a three-storey brick built office
building immediately opposite the berths.
The transit sheds were rail connected.
The tracks were owned by the Harbour
Commissioners but shunted by NCC
and GNR locomotives and crews.
This photograph shows the interior of
one of the sheds on Donegall Quay
used by the LMS.** R Welch: UFTM L4196/10

Bottom left: **Passengers from a cross-
channel steamer boarding an NCC carriage
by means of a step ladder, at Donegall
Quay in Belfast around 1935, prior to
travelling on to the Laharna Hotel at Larne.
Extra long couplings had to be used and
the vacuum bags were disconnected, to
allow the bogie carriages to go around the
tight curves on the harbour lines without
their buffers locking.** UFTM L4196/7

Photographs on the opposite page.

Top: **In this 1930s view, the turbine steamer *Princess Victoria* is seen leaving Larne Harbour at the start of its voyage to Stranraer.** UFTM WAG 2564

Bottom: **The LMS' steamer *Duke of York* on the slipway at Harland & Wolff's yard in Belfast on the day it was launched, 7th March 1935. This ship was built for the Belfast to Heysham route. During the war it was requisitioned by the Royal Navy and was renamed HMS *Duke of Wellington*. After the war it saw service on the former LMS Dun Laoghaire to Holyhead service for a time, before being sold to Greek owners in 1963.** Harland & Wolff collection: UFTM 3580

Photographs on this page.

Top: **A line-up of steamers at Donegall Quay in Belfast. The vessel nearest the camera was on the Ardrossan service, that ahead of it was bound for Glasgow. The steamer in the centre is *Duke of Argyll* on the LMS Heysham route. This was one of three ships built for the LMS by Dennys at Dumbarton in 1928. All three, the other two were the *Duke of Lancaster* and the *Duke of Rothesay*, took part in the Normandy landings.** UFTM WAG 3189

Centre: **The first turbine steamer on the Irish Sea was the *Princess Maud*, built by Dennys in 1904. She ran aground in fog at Barr's Point near Larne in 1931 and was broken up the following year.** UFTM

Right: **The SS *Scotia* was used by the LNWR on its Holyhead to Dublin service. The ship was broken up in 1928.** UFTM archive

ROYAL TRAINS

Above: **Since Queen Victoria became the first British monarch to travel by train in Ireland in 1849, all her successors have followed her lead. This is a view of the train used by the NCC for the 1924 visit by the Duke of York. The set is seen here, on a siding at York Road station, headed by U1 class 4-4-0 No 2. The train which ran from** Londonderry to Belfast on Thursday 24th July 1924, was actually hauled by No 2's sister locomotive No 1, and consisted of five bogie carriages. R Welch: UFTM L4196/11

Below left: **No 2, which acted as pilot locomotive for the 1924 royal train, had been built at York Road workshops that year and entered service in LMS crimson lake livery. No 2 is seen here, suitably decorated, for its royal duty. It was named *Glenshesk* in 1932 and withdrawn in April 1947.** R Welch: UFTM L4196/12

Below right: **On Friday 18th November 1932 the Prince of Wales visited Northern Ireland to open the new parliament building at Stormont. He travelled in a five coach special from York Road to Larne Harbour. The run took 35 minutes and the train engine, No 83, bore the Prince of Wales' feathers on its the smokebox door for the occasion and carried them for many years afterwards.**
Charles Friel collection: UFTM L4196/13

Above: **A special train was provided for the King, Queen and Princess Elizabeth when they visited Northern Ireland on 19th July 1945. However, the royal party travelled by air and the NCC had to be content with conveying the Duke of Abercorn. Mogul No 99 *King George VI* was in for overhaul at the time, so its nameplates were borrowed and put on No 101 for the day. The engine was repainted and lined in full pre-war LMS crimson lake livery for its royal train duty.** *Belfast Telegraph* collection: UFTM L3349/8

Right: **When Queen Elizabeth II and the Duke of Edinburgh visited Northern Ireland on 3rd July 1953, the UTA and GNR combined their efforts and provided a royal train composed of six GNR and four UTA coaches. All the carriages were finished in the GNR's blue and cream railcar livery and were hauled by ex- NCC Mogul No 102, in UTA lined black livery.** UFTM L1304/3

RAILWAY AIR SERVICES

By the late 1920s the 'Big Four' railway companies wished to have some involvement in the
domestic air services, in the main to protect
their express passenger services from competition from the air. Legislation passed in 1929 gave
the companies powers to operate air services.
The GWR was the pioneer, starting services in
1933. Later that year plans were made to launch
a new airline owned jointly by the four railway
companies and Imperial Airways. Railway Air
Services Ltd was set up in March 1934 and
services began later that year.

Operations on the LMS sponsored route linking London (Croydon), Belfast and Glasgow
commenced in August 1934. The NCC acted as
agents in Ulster using York Road Station and the
LMS office in the centre of Belfast as terminal
points. Passengers were discreetly weighed before
boarding. The services linked Belfast with Glasgow, Manchester, Birmingham, London and the
Isle of Man.

At first planes landed at RAF Aldergrove, but
soon transferred to Newtownards. A further
move was made to Sydenham Airport in 1938.
On 3rd July 1938 an RAS plane crashed on land-
ing at Sydenham, killing both crew. There were
fortunately no passengers on board.

The flight time between Belfast and London
was 2hr 45min. A typical return fare was £9.00,
this included the cost of road transport to and
from the centre of Belfast in a chauffeur driven
Daimler. The coming of war in 1939 initially dis-
rupted air services but for most of the war the
RAS continued to operate regular flights. Late
1945 saw the introduction of a fleet of Avro 19s
on a non-stop Croydon to Belfast service.

By 1946 the RAS was back in full operation
using ex-German Junkers Ju 52 airliners, but they
were soon replaced by Douglas DC-3 Dakotas.

British European Airways took over the RAS fleet on 1st February 1947 under a nationalisation programme, thus ending the NCC's involvement in aviation.

Pictures on page 90 - all John Stroud collection:

Top: **The LMS owned a one third share in Isle of Man Air Services. Routes linking Ulster to the IoM operated throughout the RAS era. Here, IoMAS DH.89 Dragon Rapide, G-AEAM, is seen at Liverpool Airport in May 1939.**

Centre: **De Havilland DH.89 Dragon Rapide G-ACPR** *City of Birmingham* **was one of the first aircraft acquired by the RAS in 1934.**

Bottom: **The four-engined De Havilland DH.86 Express was also used by RAS from the start. G-AEWR, named** *Venus*, **is seen at Croydon.**

Photographs on this page:

Top: **DH.86 G-ACVY** *Mercury* **is refuelling at Belfast Harbour Airport, at Sydenham, on 24th May 1939.** John Stroud collection

Right: **RAS DH.86B G-AEFH** *Neptune* **at Belfast Harbour Airport shortly after the latter was officially opened by Mrs Chamberlain, the wife of the Prime Minister, on 16th March 1938. This airport was regularly used by RAS between 1938 and 1946, at which time services were transferred to the Nutts Corner Airport.** Jack Woods collection

Below: **DH.86B Express G-AEFH** *Neptune* **is seen taking off from Belfast Harbour Airport. Then as now, the railway line to Bangor passed close to the airport perimeter. The trail of steam below this RAS aircraft is coming from a BCDR train heading for Bangor.** Jack Woods collection

THE POST-WAR ERA

Left: **With the UTA's line closures and the influx of the new WT class tanks between 1946 and 1950, many older NCC engines were withdrawn. V class 0-6-0 No 15 was built in 1923 and survived until 1961. It is seen here in UTA livery**. David Anderson

Below: **Something of the spirit of the glory days of the LMS' stewardship survived into the 1950s. In 1951, to celebrate the Festival of Britain, a new rake of carriages was built at the UTA's Duncrue Street workshops in Belfast, based on pre-war standard LMS designs. They were used on the up morning train from Derry and a late afternoon down working, both of which carried through portions for Portrush. The two workings were called, 'The Festival'. This train, headed by Mogul No 92, *The Bann*, poses here for its publicity shots at Antrim.** Reg Ludgate collection: UFTM LUD2536

NCC LOCOMOTIVES ON OTHER LINES

Above: **In the early 1950s, WT tanks Nos 7 and 10 were used by the UTA on the Bangor line, the only part of the BCDR system to escape the Authority's axe, pending the arrival of enough diesel railcars to operate the service. No 10 is seen leaving Queen's Quay on 12th August 1953 with a train for Bangor, passing withdrawn BCDR steam locomotives in the background. Strictly speaking No 10 was the last locomotive built by the LMS for the NCC, as the final eight Jeeps were built after nationalisation by British Railways.**
Reg Ludgate collection: UFTM LUD2538

Right: **Dieselisation on their own system drove many NCC engines onto former GNR lines after the remains of the GNR were nationalised on both sides of the border in 1958. Jeep No 54 and Moguls Nos 97 and 98 peer out of the former GNR roundhouse at Portadown on 26th October 1961. The W and WT classes were regular performers on the former GNR lines to Dublin, Derry and Warrenpoint in the 1960s.**
R A O'Sullivan: UFTM L4196/16

Left: **WT class tank No 53 is seen at Belfast's Great Victoria Street station with the 9.25am rugby special to Dublin on 26th June 1966. By this time the GNR lines from Portadown to Derry and from Goraghwood to Warrenpoint had been closed by the UTA and only five GNR locomotives remained in service. The whole 18 strong fleet of Jeeps survived to be taken into stock by Northern Ireland Railways when that company was formed in 1968, following the break up of the UTA.** John Lockett: UFTM L3912/2

Below: **By the mid-1960s the WTs were a common sight on the former GNR main line. No 53 again is the locomotive, here she is passing through Adelaide with a train bound for the former GNR goods yard at the Grosvenor Road in Belfast.** Midland Publishing collection

Above: **In 1966, the UTA won a contract to move over four million tons of spoil, from a quarry at Magheramorne to the shores of Belfast Lough near York Road station, to reclaim land on which a new motorway was to be built. Between December 1966 and May 1970, over 7,600 spoil trains were** run, each carrying around 600 tons in specially constructed wagons with hydraulically operated side doors to discharge the spoil. These trains, hauled by the Jeeps, kept steam alive in Ireland into the 1970s. **No 51, seen here at Greenisland, was not withdrawn until 1971.** S C Nash: UFTM L4197/11

Below: **No 53 pauses at Whitehead as railcars in NIR livery come off the single line section ahead with a Larne Harbour to York Road working.**
Midland Publishing collection

NCC SURVIVORS

Above: **Jeep No 4, owned by the Railway Preservation Society of Ireland, hauls the Society's regular summer service, the 'Portrush Flyer', out of a much truncated York Road, in the 1970s. The motorway on the left of the picture was that which No 4 and her sisters helped to build in their last years in service.** Charles Friel

Left: **Old rivals in partnership. The railway collection of the former Belfast Transport Museum is now housed in the railway gallery at the Ulster Folk & Transport Museum at Cultra. GNR S class 4-4-0 No 171 *Slieve Gullion* has brought a carriage to the museum on 26th September 1993. To enable it to be positioned in the gallery, which is linked by a spur to the Bangor line, NCC 4-4-0 No 74, *Dunluce Castle*, has been shunted out of the museum and on to the running line. Who knows, a crimson-liveried LMS 4-4-0, hauling a passenger train, might yet be seen again on Irish rails in the twenty-first century ?** Charles Friel